INSIDE MAHATMA'S MIND

Famous Speeches & Thoughts of Gandhi

Published by
Rupa Publications India Pvt. Ltd 2019
7/16, Ansari Road, Daryaganj
New Delhi 110002

Sales Centres:

Allahabad Bengaluru Chennai
Hyderabad Jaipur Kathmandu
Kolkata Mumbai

ISBN: 978-93-5333-678-3

First impression 2019

10 9 8 7 6 5 4 3 2 1

Printed at HT Media Ltd., Gr. Noida

INSIDE MAHATMA'S MIND

Mahatma Gandhi (2 October 1869–30 January 1948), born as Mohandas Karamchand Gandhi, was an Indian lawyer, politician, writer and social activist. Due to his active involvement in the nationalist movement against British rule in India, Gandhi came to be known as the Father of the Nation, or Bapu ('Bapu' being the Indian word for 'father').

Gandhi's doctrine of non-violent protest (also known as satyagraha) is recognized worldwide. His non-violent non-cooperation movement against the British government in India boycotted not only British goods but also British-run or -supported institutions. He also set the tone for swaraj, or self-governance, which was the underlying principle of the freedom movement. Gandhi's Salt March (also known as the Dandi March) and the Quit India Movement are two watersheds in India's struggle for Independence.

Contents

FAMOUS SPEECHES

1. Reception in Madras 3
2. Gandhi's Speech at Banaras Hindu University (BHU), 1916 7
3. Statement during the Great Trial of 1922 17
4. On the Eve of the Historic Dandi March 27
5. Speech at the Round Table Conference, 1931 31
6. The Quit India Speeches, 1942 36
7. Speech before Inter-Asian Relations Conference, 1947 64
8. On Kashmir 69
9. Speech on the Eve of the Last Fast, 1948 73

THOUGHTS OF MAHATMA GANDHI

10. Non-violence and World Crisis 79
11. Non-violence vs Violence 84
12. Religion vs No Religion 90
13. The Doctrine of the Sword 93
14. Resistance to Aggression 98
15. The Way of Ahimsa 101
16. Non-violent Resistance 104
17. Never Doubt Non-violence 106
18. The Choice before India 109
19. No Imitation of the West 111
20. Alternative to War 114
21. India and the Creed of Non-violence 115
22. Non-violence of the Brave 116
23. The Significance of Non-violence for India 117

24. India's Duty 118
25. The Way to Peace 120
26. What Should a Neutral State Do? 121
27. Great Power and Disarmament 123
28. Gangsterism vs Non-violence 124
29. Non-violent Alternative 126
30. Peace through Love 128
31. Enduring Peace 129
32. No 'Appeasement' 131
33. Non-violent Society 132
34. End to War 133
35. Pacifism and Pacifists 135
36. The Gospel of Non-violence 136
37. Character of Non-violence 138
38. Changeless Creed 140
39. Faith in God 141
40. Religious Basis 143
41. Hinduism's Unique Contribution 145
42. The Koran and Non-violence 146
43. No Matter of Diet 148
44. Road to Truth 149
45. No Cover for Cowardice 151
46. Humility Essential 154
47. Active Force 156
48. Matchless Bravery 158
49. Exercise in Faith 159
50. A Science 160
51. The Deed, not Doer 161
52. Training for Non-violence 163
53. Fearlessness: the Prerequisite 164
54. Non-violence of the Brave 166
55. Application of Non-violence 168

56. Universality of Non-violence 169
57. Cultivation of Non-violence 170
58. Use on Mass Scale 171
59. Efficacy 172
60. The Non-violent Society 173
61. The Government 174
62. Anarchy 175
63. Democracy and Non-violence 176
64. Use of Power 178
65. The Non-violent State 180
66. Political Power 181
67. Capitalism: a Trusteeship 182
68. Non-violent Swaraj 184
69. Decentralization 186
70. Modern State 187
71. Violence and Terrorism 188
72. No Faith in Violence 189
73. The Revolutionary 190
74. Prevention of Brutalization 192
75. Heroes of History 194
76. Revolution Suicidal 195
77. Between Cowardice and Violence 197
78. No Cowardice 199
79. Self-defence by Violence 201
80. India and the Non-violent Way 203
81. Mere Passive Resistance 204
82. Crime and Punishment 208
83. The Gospel of the Charkha 210
84. Message of the Charkha 212
85. Return to Simplicity 214
86. Wheel of Life 215

Famous Speeches

1

Reception in Madras

This speech was in reply to the welcome address read by Mr G.A. Natesan on behalf of the Indian South African League, at a meeting at the Victoria Public Hall, Madras, on 21 April 1915, with Dr (Sir) Subramania Iyer in the Chair.

(21 April 1915)

Mr Chairman and friends,

On behalf of my wife and myself, I am deeply grateful for the great honour, that you here, and Madras, and may I say, this Presidency, have done to us and the affection that has been lavished upon us in this great and enlightened—not benighted—Presidency.

If there is anything that we have deserved, as has been stated in this beautiful address, I can only say I lay it at the feet of my Master under whose inspiration I have been working all this time under exile in South Africa. (Hear, hear).

In so far as the sentiments expressed in this address are merely prophetic. Sir, I accept them as a blessing and as a prayer from you and from this great meeting that both my wife and I myself may possess the power, the inclination and the life to dedicate whatever we may develop in this sacred land of ours to the service of the Motherland. (Cheers).

It is no wonder that we have come to Madras. As my friend, Mr Natesan, will perhaps tell you, we have been overdue and we have neglected Madras. But we have done nothing of the kind. We know that we had a corner in your hearts and we knew that you will not misjudge us if we did not hasten to Madras before going to the other presidencies and to other towns. But, Sir, if one-tenth of the language that has been used in this address is deserved by us, what language do you propose to use for those who have lost their lives, and therefore finished their work on behalf of your suffering countrymen in South Africa? What language do you propose to use for Nagappan and Narayanaswamy, lads of 17 or 18 years, who braved in simple faith all the trials, all the sufferings, and all the indignities for the sake of the honour of the Motherland (Cheers).

What language do you propose to use with reference to Valliamma, that sweet girl of 17 years who was discharged from Maritzburg prison, skin and bone suffering from fever to which she succumbed after about a month's time (Cries of shame).

It was the Madrasis, who of all the Indians, were singled out by the great Divinity that rules over us for this great work. Do you know that in the great city of Johannesburg, the Madrasis look on a Madrasi as dishonoured if he has not passed through the jails once or twice during this terrible crisis that your countrymen in South Africa went through during these eight long years? You have said that I inspired these great men and women, but I cannot accept that proposition. It was they, the simple-minded folk, who worked away in faith, never expecting the slightest reward, who inspired me, who kept me on the proper level, and who inspired me by their great sacrifice, by their great faith, by their great trust in the great God, to do the work that I was able to do. (Cheers).

It is my misfortune that my wife and I have been obliged to work in the limelight, and you have magnified out of all proportion (cries of 'No? No?') this little work we have been able to do. Believe me, my dear friends, that if you consider, whether in India or in South Africa, it is possible for us, poor mortals—the same individuals, the same stuff of which you are made—if you consider that it is possible for us to do anything whatsoever without your assistance and without your doing the same thing that we would be prepared to do, you are lost, and we are also lost, and our services will be in vain; I do not for one moment believe that the inspiration was given by us. The inspiration was given by them to us, and we were able to be interpreters between the powers who called themselves the governors and those men for whom redress was so necessary. We were simply links between those two parties and nothing more. It was my duty, having received the education that was given to me by my parents to interpret what was going on in our midst to those simple folk, and they rose to the occasion. They realized the might of religious force, and it was they who inspired us, and let them who have finished their work, and who have died for you and me, let them inspire you and us. We are still living and who knows whether the devil will not possess us tomorrow and we shall not forsake the post of duty before any new danger that may face us.

An old man of 75 from the United Provinces, Harbart Singh, has also joined the majority and died in jail in South Africa; and he deserved the crown that you would seek to impose upon us. These young men deserve all the adjectives that you have so affectionately, but blindly lavished upon us.

It was not only the Hindus who struggled, but there were Mohamedans, Parsis and Christians, and almost every part of India was represented in the struggle. They realized the common danger, and they realized also what their destiny was as Indians, and it was they, and they alone, who matched the soul forces against the physical forces. (Loud applause)

2

Gandhi's Speech at Banaras Hindu University (BHU), 1916

This was on the occasion of the opening of Banaras Hindu University (BHU). Pandit Malaviya had invited Gandhiji to speak on the occasion and Lord Hardinge, the viceroy, had come specially to lay the foundation stone of the university. Since Lord Hardinge was the special guest, the entire city was in a state of siege. Extra precautions were taken to offer him protection and there were police force in every nook and corner of the city.

(4 February 1916)

Eminent persons from all over India had come. Many of them delivered addresses. On 4 February 1916, it was Gandhiji's turn to address the audience, mostly consisting of impressionable youths. A galaxy of princes, bedecked and bejeweled, had occupied the dais. The Maharaja of Darbhanga was in the Chair.

Gandhiji, who was clad in a short, coarse dhoti, Kathiawadi cloak and turban, rose to speak. The police precautions and the luxury around him hurt him deeply. Turning to the audience, Gandhiji said that he wanted to think audibly—speak without reserve:

I wish to tender my humble apology for the long delay that took place before I was able to reach this place. And you will readily accept the apology when I tell you that I am not responsible for the delay nor is any human agency responsible for it. The fact is that I am like an animal on show, and my keepers in their overkindness always manage to neglect a necessary chapter in this life, and that is pure accident. In this case, they did not provide for the series of accidents that happened to us—to me, keepers, and my carriers. Hence this delay!

Friends, under the influence of the matchless eloquence of Mrs Besant, who has just sat down, pray, do not believe that our university has become a finished product, and that all the young men who are to come to the university, that has yet to rise and come into existence, have also come and returned from it finished citizens of a great empire. Do not go away with any such impression, and if you, the student world to which my remarks are supposed to be addressed this evening, consider for one moment that the spiritual life, for which this country is noted and for which this country has no rival, can be transmitted through the lip, pray, believe me, you are wrong. You will never be able merely through the lip to give the message that India, I hope, will one day deliver to the world. I myself have been fed up with speeches and lectures. I except the lectures that have been delivered here during the last two days from this category, because they are necessary. But I do venture to suggest to you that we have now reached almost the end of our resources in speech-making; it is not enough that our ears are feasted, that our eyes are feasted, but it is necessary that our hearts have got to be touched and that our hands and feet have got to be moved.

We have been told during the last two days how necessary it is, if we are to retain our hold upon the simplicity of Indian character; that our hands and feet should move in unison with our hearts. But this is only by way of preface. I wanted to say it is a matter of deep humiliation and shame for us that I am compelled this evening under the shadow of this great college, in this sacred city, to address my countrymen in a language that is foreign to me. I know that if I was appointed an examiner, to examine all those who have been attending during these two days this series of lectures, most of those who might be examined upon these lectures, would fail. And why? Because they have not been touched.

I was present at the sessions of the great Congress in the month of December. There was a much vaster audience, and will you believe me when I tell you that the only speeches that touched the huge audience in Bombay were the speeches that were delivered in Hindustani? In Bombay, mind you, not in Banaras, where everybody speaks Hindi. But between the vernaculars of the Bombay Presidency on the one hand and Hindi on the other, no such great dividing line exists—as there does between English and the sister language of India; and the Congress audience was better able to follow the speakers in Hindi. I am hoping that this university will see to it that the youths who come to it will receive their instruction through the medium of their vernaculars. Our languages are the reflection of ourselves, and if you tell me that our languages are too poor to express the best thought, then say that the sooner we are wiped out of existence, the better for us. Is there a man who dreams that English can ever become the national language of India? Why this handicap on the nation? Just consider for one moment what an equal race our lads have to run with every English lad.

I had the privilege of a close conversation with some Poona professors. They assured me that every Indian youth, because he reached his knowledge through the English language, lost at least six precious years of his life. Multiply that by the numbers of students turned out by our schools and colleges, and find out for yourselves how many thousand years have been lost to the nation. The charge against us is that we have no initiative. How can we have any, if we are to devote the precious years of our life to the mastery of a foreign tongue? We fail in this attempt also. Was it possible for any speaker yesterday and today to impress his audience as was possible for Mr Higginbotham? It was not the fault of the previous speakers that they could not engage the audience. They had more than substance enough for us in their addresses. But their addresses could not go home to us. I have heard it said that after all it is English-educated India which is leading and which is doing all the things for the nation. It would be monstrous if it were otherwise. The only education we receive is English education. Surely we must show something for it. But suppose that we had been receiving during the past fifty years education through our vernaculars, what should we have today? We should have today a free India, we should have our educated men, not as if they were foreigners in their own land but speaking to the heart of the nation; they would be working amongst the poorest of the poor, and whatever they would have gained during these fifty years would be a heritage for the nation. Today, even our wives are not the sharers in our best thought. Look at Professor Bose and Professor Ray and their brilliant researches. Is it not a shame that their researches are not the common property of the masses?

Let us now turn to another subject.

The Congress has passed a resolution about self-government, and I have no doubt that the All India Congress Committee and the Muslim League will do their duty and come forward with some tangible suggestions. But I, for one, must frankly confess that I am not so much interested in what they will be able to produce, as I am interested in anything that the student world is going to produce or the masses are going to produce. No paper contribution will ever give us self-government. No amount of speeches will ever make us fit for self-government. It is only our conduct that will fit us for it. And how are we trying to govern ourselves?

I want to think audibly this evening. I do not want to make a speech and if you find me this evening speaking without reserve, pray, consider that you are only sharing the thoughts of a man who allows himself to think audibly, and if you think that I seem to transgress the limits that courtesy imposes upon me, pardon me for the liberty I may be taking. I visited the Vishwanath Temple last evening, and as I was walking through those lanes, these were the thoughts that touched me. If a stranger dropped from above on to this great temple, and he had to consider what we as Hindus were, would he not be justified in condemning us? Is not this great temple a reflection of our own character? I speak feelingly, as a Hindu. Is it right that the lanes of our sacred temple should be as dirty as they are? The houses round about are built anyhow. The lanes are tortuous and narrow. If even our temples are not models of roominess and cleanliness, what can our self-government be? Shall our temples be abodes of holiness, cleanliness and peace as soon as the English have retired from India, either of their own pleasure or by compulsion, bag and baggage?

I entirely agree with the president of the Congress that before we think of self-government, we shall have to do the necessary plodding. In every city, there are two divisions: the cantonment and the city proper. The city mostly is a stinking den. But we are a people unused to city life. But if we want city life, we cannot reproduce the easy-going hamlet life. It is not comforting to think that people walk about the streets of Indian Bombay under the perpetual fear of dwellers in the storeyed building spitting upon them. I do a great deal of railway traveling. I observe the difficulty of third-class passengers. But the railway administration is by no means to blame for all their hard lot. We do not know the elementary laws of cleanliness. We spit anywhere on the carriage floor, irrespective of the thoughts that it is often used as sleeping space. We do not trouble ourselves as to how we use it; the result is indescribable filth in the compartment. The so-called better-class passengers overawe their less-fortunate brethren. Among them I have seen the student world also; sometimes they behave no better. They can speak English and they have worn Norfolk jackets and, therefore, claim the right to force their way in and command seating accommodation.

I have turned the searchlight all over, and as you have given me the privilege of speaking to you, I am laying my heart bare. Surely we must set these things right in our progress towards self-government. I now introduce you to another scene. His Highness the Maharaja, who presided yesterday over our deliberations, spoke about the poverty of India. Other speakers laid great stress upon it. But what did we witness in the great pandal in which the foundation ceremony was performed by the viceroy? Certainly a most gorgeous show, an exhibition of jewellery, which made a splendid feast for the eyes of the greatest jeweler who chose to come from Paris. I compare with the richly bedecked noblemen the millions of the poor. And I feel like saying to these noblemen, 'There is no salvation for India unless you strip yourselves of this jewellery and hold it in trust for your countrymen in India.' I am sure it is not the desire of the King-Emperor or Lord Hardinge that in order to show the truest loyalty to our King-Emperor, it is necessary for us to ransack our jewellery boxes and to appear bedecked from top to toe. I would undertake, at the peril of my life, to bring to you a message from King George himself that he excepts nothing of the kind.

Sir, whenever I hear of a great palace rising in any great city of India, be it in British India or be it in India which is ruled by our great chiefs, I become jealous at once, and say, 'Oh, it is the money that has come from the agriculturists.' Over 75 per cent of the population is agriculturists and Mr Higginbotham told us last night in his own felicitous language, that they are the men who grow two blades of grass in the place of one. But there cannot be much spirit of self-government about us, if we take away or allow others to take away from them almost the whole of the results of their labour. Our salvation can only come through the farmer. Neither the lawyers, nor the doctors, nor the rich landlords are going to secure it.

Now, last but not least, it is my bounden duty to refer to what agitated our minds during these two or three days. All of us have had many anxious moments while the viceroy was going through the streets of Banaras. There were detectives stationed in many places. We were horrified. We asked ourselves, 'Why this distrust?' Is it not better that even Lord Hardinge should die than live a living death? But a representative of a mighty sovereign may not. He might find it necessary to impose these detectives on us? We may foam, we may fret, we may resent, but let us not forget that India of today, in her impatience, has produced an army of anarchists. I myself am an anarchist, but of another type. But there is a class of anarchists amongst us, and if I was able to reach this class, I would say to them that their anarchism has no room in India, if India is to conqueror. It is a sign of fear. If we trust and fear God, we shall have to fear no one, not the maharajas, not the viceroys, not the detectives, not even King George.

I honour the anarchist for his love of the country. I honour him for his bravery in being willing to die for his country; but I ask him—is killing honourable? Is the dagger of an assassin a fit precursor of an honourable death? I deny it. There is no warrant for such methods in any scriptures. If I found it necessary for the salvation of India that the English should retire, that they should be driven out, I would not hesitate to declare that they would have to go, and I hope I would be prepared to die in defence of that belief. That would, in my opinion, be an honourable death. The bomb-thrower creates secret plots, is afraid to come out into the open, and when caught, pays the penalty of misdirected zeal.

I have been told, 'Had we not done this, had some people not thrown bombs, we should never have gained what we have got with reference to the Partition movement.' (Mrs Besant: 'Please stop it.')

This was what I said in Bengal when Mr Lyon presided at the meeting. I think what I am saying is necessary. If I am told to stop, I shall obey.

(Turning to the chairman) I await your orders. If you consider that by my speaking as I am, I am not serving the country and the empire, I shall certainly stop. (Cries of 'Go on.') (The Chairman: 'Please, explain your object.')

I am simply...(another interruption).

My friends, please do not resent this interruption. If Mrs Besant this evening suggests that I should stop, she does so because she loves India so well, and she considers that I am erring in thinking audibly before you young men. But even so, I simply say this; that I want to purge India of this atmosphere of suspicion on either side, if we are to reach our goal; we should have an empire which is to be based upon mutual love and mutual trust. Is it not better that we talk under the shadow of this college than that we should be talking irresponsibly in our homes? I consider that it is much better that we talk about these things more openly. I have done so with excellent results, before now. I know that there is nothing that the students do not know. I am, therefore, turning the searchlight towards ourselves. I hold the name of my country so dear to me that I exchange these thoughts with you, and submit to you that there is no room for anarchism in India. Let us frankly and openly say whatever we want to say to our rulers, and face the consequences if what we have to say does not please them. But let us not abuse. I was talking the other day to a member of the much-abused Civil Service. I have not very much in common with the members of that Service, but I could not help admiring the manner in which he was speaking to me. He said: 'Mr Gandhi, do you for one moment suppose that all we, Civil Servants, are a bad lot, that we want to oppress the people whom we have come to govern?' 'No,' I said. 'Then, if you get an opportunity, put in a word for the much-abused Civil Service.' And I am here to put in that word. Yes, many members of the Indian Civil

Service are most decidedly overbearing; they are tyrannical, at times thoughtless. Many other adjectives may be used. I grant all these things and I grant also that after having lived in India for a certain number of years, some of them become somewhat degraded. But what does that signify? They were gentlemen before they came here, and if they have lost some of the moral fiber, it is a reflection upon ourselves.

Just think out for yourselves—if a man who was good yesterday has become bad after having come in contact with me, is he responsible that he has deteriorated or am I? The atmosphere of sycophancy and falsity that surrounds them on their coming to India demoralizes them, as it would many of us. It is well to take the blame sometimes. If we are to receive self-government, we shall have to take it. We shall never be granted self-government. Look at the history of the British empire and the British nation; freedom loving as it is, it will not be a party to give freedom to a people who will not take it themselves. Learn your lesson if you wish to from the Boer War. Those who were enemies of that empire only a few years ago have now become friends...

(At this point, there was an interruption and a movement on the platform to leave. The speech, therefore, ended abruptly.)

3

Statement during the Great Trial of 1922

This was a historic trial of Mahatma Gandhi and Shri Shankarlal Ghelabhai Banker, editor, printer and publisher of Young India. The trial was conducted on charges under Section 124A of the Indian Penal Code, and was held on Saturday, 18 March 1922, before Mr C.N. Broomfield, I.C.S., District and Sessions Judge, Ahmedabad.

(18 March 1922)

Sir J.T. Strangman, Advocate-General, with Rao Bahadur Girdharlal Uttamram, Public Prosecutor of Ahmedabad, appeared for the Crown. Mr A.C. Wild, Remembrancer of Legal Affairs, was also present. Mahatma Gandhi and Shri Shankarlal Banker were undefended.

Among the members of the public who were present on the occasion were: Kasturba Gandhi, Sarojini Naidu, Pandit M.M. Malaviya, Shri N.C. Kelkar, Smt J.B. Petit and Smt Anasuyaben Sarabhai.

The Judge, who took his seat at 12 noon, said that there was a slight mistake in the charges framed, which he corrected. The charges were then read out by the Registrar. These charges were of 'bringing or attempting to excite disaffection towards His Majesty's government established by law in British India, and thereby committing offences punishable under Section 124A of the Indian Penal Code,' the offences being in three articles published in *Young India* of September 29 and December 15 of 1921, and February 23 of 1922. The offending articles were then read out: first of them was, 'Tampering with Loyalty'; and second, 'The Puzzle and its Solution,' and the last was 'Shaking the Manes.'

The Judge said that the law required that the charges should not be read out but explained. In this case, it would not be necessary for him to say much by way of explanation. The charge in each case was that of bringing or attempting to excite into hatred or contempt or exciting or attempting to excite disaffection towards His Majesty's Government, established by law in British India. Both the accused were charged with the three offences under Section 124A, contained in the articles read out, written by Mahatma Gandhi and printed by Shri Banker.

The charges having been read out, the Judge called upon the accused to plead to the charges. He asked Gandhiji whether he pleaded guilty or claimed to be tried.

Gandhiji said: 'I plead guilty to all the charges. I observe that the King's name has been omitted from the charge, and it has been properly omitted.'

The Judge asked Shri Banker the same question and he too readily pleaded guilty.

The Judge wished to give his verdict immediately after Gandhiji had pleaded guilty, but Sir Strangman insisted that the procedure should be carried out in full. The Advocate-General requested the Judge to take into account 'the occurrences in

Bombay, Malabar and Chauri Chaura, leading to rioting and murder'. He admitted, indeed, that 'in these articles, you find that non-violence is insisted upon as an item of the campaign and of the creed', but the added 'of what value is it to insist on non-violence, if incessantly you preach disaffection towards the Government and hold it up as a treacherous Government, and if you openly and deliberately seek to instigate others to overthrow it?' These were the circumstances which he asked the Judge to take into account in passing sentence on the accused.

As regards Shri Banker, the second accused, the offence was lesser. He did the publication but did not write. Sir Strangman's instructions were that Shri Banker was a man of means and he requested the court to impose a substantial fine in addition to such term of imprisonment as might be inflicted upon.

Court: Mr Gandhi, do you wish to make any statement on the question of sentence?

Gandhiji: I would like to make a statement.

Court: Could you give me in writing to put it on record?

Gandhiji: I shall give it as soon as I finish it.

(Gandhiji then made the following oral statement followed by a written statement that he read.)

Before I read this statement, I would like to state that I entirely endorse the learned Advocate-General's remarks in connection with my humble self. I think that he has made, because it is very true and I have no desire whatsoever to conceal from this court the fact that to preach disaffection towards the existing system of government has become almost a passion with me, and the Advocate-General is entirely in the right when he says that my preaching of disaffection did not commence with my connection with *Young India,* but that it commenced much earlier, and in the statement that I am about to read, it will be my painful duty to admit before this court that it commenced much earlier than the period stated by the Advocate-General. It is a painful duty with me, but I have to discharge that duty knowing the responsibility that rests upon my shoulders, and I wish to endorse all the blame that the learned Advocate-General has thrown on my shoulders in connection with the Bombay occurrences, Madras occurrences and the Chauri Chaura occurrences. Thinking over these things deeply and sleeping over them night after night, it is impossible for me to dissociate myself from the diabolical crimes of Chauri Chaura or the mad outrages of Bombay. He is quite right when he says, that as a man of responsibility, a man having received a fair share of education, having had a fair share of experience of this world, I should have known the consequences of every one of my acts. I know them. I knew that I was playing with fire. I ran the risk and if I was set free, I would still do the same. I have felt it this morning that I would have failed in my duty, if I did not say what I said here just now.

I wanted to avoid violence. Non-violence is the first article of my faith. It is also the last article of my creed. But I had to make my choice. I had either to submit to a system which I considered had done an irreparable harm to my country, or incur the risk of the mad fury of my people bursting forth when they understood the truth from my lips. I know that my people have sometimes gone mad. I am deeply sorry for it and

I am, therefore, here to submit not to a light penalty but to the highest penalty. I do not ask for mercy. I do not plead any extenuating act. I am here, therefore, to invite and cheerfully submit to the highest penalty that can be inflicted upon me for what in law is a deliberate crime, and what appears to me to be the highest duty of a citizen. The only course open to you, the Judge, is, as I am going to say in my statement, either to resign your post, or inflict on me the severest penalty if you believe that the system and law you are assisting to administer are good for the people. I do not except that kind of conversion. But by the time I have finished with my statement, you will have a glimpse of what is raging within my breast to run this maddest risk which a sane man can run.

(He then read out the written statement) I owe it perhaps to the Indian public and to the public in England, to placate which this prosecution is mainly taken up, that I should explain why from a staunch loyalist and co-operator, I have become an uncompromising disaffectionist and non-cooperator. To the court, too, I should say why I plead guilty to the charge of promoting disaffection towards the government established by law in India.

My public life began in 1893 in South Africa in troubled weather. My first contact with British authority in that country was not of a happy character. I discovered that as a man and an Indian, I had no rights. More correctly, I discovered that I had no rights as a man because I was an Indian.

But I was not baffled. I thought that this treatment of Indians was an excrescence upon a system that was intrinsically and mainly good. I gave the government my voluntary and hearty co-operation, criticizing it freely where I felt it was faulty but never wishing its destruction.

Consequently, when the existence of the Empire was threatened in 1899 by the Boer challenge, I offered my services to it, raised a volunteer ambulance corps and served at several actions that took place for the relief of Ladysmith. Similarly in 1906, at the time of the Zulu 'revolt', I raised a stretcher-bearer party and served till the end of the 'rebellion'. On both the occasions, I received medals and was even mentioned in dispatches. For my work in South Africa, I was given by Lord Hardinge a Kaisar-i-Hind gold medal. When the war broke out in 1914 between England and Germany, I raised volunteer ambulance cars in London, consisting of the then resident Indians in London, chiefly students. Its work was acknowledged by the authorities to be valuable. Lastly, in India, when a special appeal was made at the War Conference in Delhi in 1918 by Lord Chelmsford for recruits, I struggled at the cost of my health to raise a corps in Kheda, and the response was being made when the hostilities ceased and orders were received that no more recruits were wanted. In all these efforts at service, I was actuated by the belief that it was possible by such services to gain a status of full equality in the Empire for my countrymen.

The first shock came in the shape of the Rowlatt Act—a law designed to rob the people of all real freedom. I felt called upon to lead an intensive agitation against it. Then followed the Punjab horrors, beginning with the massacre at Jallianwala Bagh and culminating in crawling orders, public flogging and other indescribable humiliations. I discovered too that the plighted word of the prime minister to the Mussalmans of India regarding the integrity of Turkey and the holy places of Islam was not likely to be fulfilled. But in spite of the forebodings and the grave warnings of friends, at the Amritsar

Congress in 1919, I fought for co-operation and working of the Montagu-Chelmsford reforms, hoping that the prime minister would redeem his promise to the Indian Mussalmans, that the Punjab wound would be healed, and that the reforms, inadequate and unsatisfactory though they were, marked a new era of hope in the life of India.

But all that hope was shattered. The Khilafat promise was not to be redeemed. The Punjab crime was whitewashed and most culprits went not only unpunished but remained in service, and some continued to draw pensions from the Indian revenue and in some cases were even rewarded. I saw too that not only did the reforms not mark a change of heart, but they were only a method of further draining India of her wealth and of prolonging her servitude.

I came reluctantly to the conclusion that the British connection had made India more helpless than she ever was before, politically and economically. A disarmed India has no power of resistance against any aggressor if she wanted to engage in an armed conflict with him. So much is this the case that some of our best men consider that India must take generations, before she can achieve Dominion Status. She has become so poor that she has little power of resisting famines. Before the British advent, India spun and wove in her millions of cottages, just the supplement she needed for adding to her meagre agricultural resources. This cottage industry—so vital for India's existence—has been ruined by incredibly heartless and inhuman processes as described by English witness. Little do town-dwellers know how the semi-starved masses of India are slowly sinking to lifelessness! Little do they know that their miserable comfort represents the brokerage they get for their work they do for the foreign exploiter, that the profits and the brokerage are sucked from the masses. Little do they realize that the government established by law in British India is carried on for this exploitation of the masses! No sophistry, no jugglery in figures, can explain away the evidence that the skeletons in many villages present to the naked eye. I have no doubt whatsoever that both England and the town-dweller of India will have to answer, if there is a God above, for this crime against humanity, which is perhaps unequalled in history. The law itself in this country has been used to serve the foreign exploiter. My unbiased examination of the Punjab Marital Law cases has led me to believe that at least 95 per cent of convictions were wholly bad. My experience of political cases in India leads me to the conclusion, in nine out of every ten, the condemned men were totally innocent. Their crime consisted in the love of their country. In ninety-nine cases out of hundred, justice has been denied to Indians as against Europeans in the courts of India. This is not an exaggerated picture. It is the experience of almost every Indian who has had anything to do with such cases. In my opinion, the administration of the law is thus prostituted, consciously or unconsciously, for the benefit of the exploiter.

The greater misfortune is that the Englishmen and their Indian associates in the administration of the country do not know that they are engaged in the crime I have attempted to describe. I am satisfied that many Englishmen and Indian officials honestly believe that they are administering one of the best systems devised in the world, and that India is making steady, though, slow progress. They do not know, a subtle but effective system of terrorism and an organized display of force on the one hand, and the deprivation of all powers of retaliation or self-defence on the other, have emasculated the people and induced in them the habit of simulation. This awful habit has added to the ignorance and the self-deception of the administrators. Section 124A, under which I am happily charged, is perhaps the prince among the political sections of the Indian Penal Code designed to suppress the liberty of the citizen. Affection cannot be manufactured or regulated by law. If one has no affection for a person or system, one should be free to give the fullest expression to his disaffection, so long as he does not contemplate, promote or incite to violence. But the section under which Mr Banker and I are charged is one under which mere promotion of disaffection is a crime. I have studied some of the cases tried under it; I know that some of the most loved of India's patriots have been convicted under it. I consider it a privilege, therefore, to be charged under that section. I have endeavored to give in their briefest outline the reasons for my disaffection. I have no personal ill will against any single administrator, much less can I have any disaffection towards the King's person. But I hold it to be a virtue to be disaffected towards a government which in its totality has done more harm to India than any previous system. India is less manly under the British rule than she ever was before. Holding such a belief, I consider it to be a sin to have affection for the system. And it has been a precious privilege for me to be able to write what I have in the various articles tendered in evidence against me.

In fact, I believe that I have rendered a service to India and England by showing in non-cooperation the way out of the unnatural state in which both are living. In my opinion, non-cooperation with evil is as much a duty as is cooperation with good. But in the past, non-cooperation has been deliberately expressed in violence to the evil-doer. I am endeavouring to show to my countrymen that violent non-cooperation only multiples evil, and that as evil can only be sustained by violence, withdrawal of support of evil requires complete abstention from violence. Non-violence implies voluntary submission to the penalty for non-cooperation with evil. I am here, therefore, to invite and submit cheerfully to the highest penalty that can be inflicted upon me for what in law is deliberate crime, and what appears to me to be the highest duty of a citizen. The only course open to you, the Judge and the assessors, is either to resign your posts and thus dissociate yourselves from evil, if you feel that the law you are called upon to administer is an evil, and that in reality I am innocent, or to inflict on me the severest penalty, if you believe that the system and the law you are assisting to administer are good for the people of this country, and that my activity is, therefore, injurious to the public weal.

4

On the Eve of the Historic Dandi March

This was a memorable speech delivered by Gandhiji on 11 March 1930. The crowd that had swelled to 10,000 was waiting in anticipation and Gandhiji, after his evening prayers, delivered a historic speech that heralded the beginning of Dandi March.

(11 March 1930)

In all probability, this will be my last speech to you. Even if the government allows me to march tomorrow morning, this will be my last speech on the sacred banks of the Sabarmati. Possibly these may be the last words of my life here.

I have already told you yesterday what I had to say. Today, I shall confine myself to what you should do after my companions and I are arrested. The programme of the march to Jalalpur must be fulfilled as originally settled. The enlistment of the volunteers for this purpose should be confined to Gujarat only. From what I have seen and heard during the last fortnight, I am inclined to believe that the stream of civil resisters will flow unbroken.

But let there be not a semblance of breach of peace, even after all of us have been arrested. We have resolved to utilize all our resources in the pursuit of an exclusively non-violent struggle. Let no one commit a wrong in anger. This is my hope and prayer. I wish these words of mine reached every nook and corner of the land. My task shall be done if I perish and so do my comrades. It will then be for the Working Committee of the Congress to show you the way and it will be up to you to follow its lead. So long as I have reached Jalalpur, let nothing be done in contravention to the authority vested in me by the Congress. But once I am arrested, the whole responsibility shifts to the Congress. No one who believes in non-violence, as a creed, need, therefore, sit still. My compact with the Congress ends as soon as I am arrested. In that case, volunteers. Wherever possible, civil disobedience of salt should be started. These laws can be violated in three ways. It is an offence to manufacture salt wherever there are facilities for doing so. The possession and sale of contraband salt, which includes natural salt or salt earth, is also an offence. The purchasers of such salt will be equally guilty. To carry away the natural salt deposits on the seashore is likewise violation of law. So is the hawking of such salt. In short, you may choose any one or all of these devices to break the salt monopoly.

We are, however, not to be content with this alone. There is no ban by the Congress and wherever the local workers have self-confidence, other suitable measures may be adopted. I stress only one condition, namely, let our pledge of truth and non-violence as the only means for the attainment of swaraj (self-rule) be faithfully kept. For the rest, everyone has a free hand. But, that does not give a license to all and sundry to carry on their own responsibility. Wherever there are local leaders, their orders should be obeyed by the people. Where there are no leaders and only a handful of men have faith in the programme, they may do what they can, if they have enough self-confidence. They have a right, nay it is their duty, to do so. The history of the world is full of instances of men who rose to leadership, by sheer force of self-confidence, bravery and tenacity. We, too, if we sincerely aspire to swaraj and are impatient to attain it, should have similar self-confidence. Our ranks will swell and our hearts strengthen, as the number of our arrests by the government increases.

Much can be done in many other ways besides these. The liquor and foreign cloth shops can be picketed. We can refuse to pay taxes if we have the requisite strength. The lawyers can give up practice. The public can boycott the law courts by refraining from litigation. Government servants can resign from their posts. In the midst of the despair reigning all round, people quake with fear of losing employment. Such men are unfit for swaraj. But why this despair? The number of government servants in the country does not exceed a few hundred thousand. What about the rest? Where are they to go? Even free India will not be able to accommodate a greater number of public servants. A collector then will not need the number of servants he has got today. He will be his own servant. Our starving millions can by no means afford this enormous expenditure. If, therefore, we are sensible enough, let us bid good-bye to government employment, no matter if it is the post of a judge or a peon. Let all who are co-operating with the government in one way or another—be it by paying taxes, keeping titles or sending children to official schools, etc.—withdraw their co-operation in all or as many ways as possible. Then there are women who can stand shoulder to shoulder with men in this struggle.

You may take it as my will. It was the message that I desired to impart to you before starting on the march or for the jail. I wish that there should be no suspension or abandonment of the war that commences tomorrow morning or earlier, if I am arrested before that time. I shall eagerly await the news that ten batches are ready as soon as my batch is arrested. I believe there are men in India to complete the work begun by me. I have faith in the righteousness of our cause and the purity of our weapons. And where the means are clean, there God is undoubtedly present with His blessings. And where these three combine, there defeat is an impossibility. A satyagrahi, whether free or incarcerated, is ever victorious. He is vanquished only when he forsakes truth and non-violence and turns a deaf ear to the inner voice. If, therefore, there is such a thing as defeat for even a satyagrahi, he alone is the cause of it. God bless you all and keep off all obstacles from the path in the struggle that begins tomorrow.

5

Speech at the Round Table Conference, 1931

In response to the inadequacy of the Simon Report, the Labour Government, which had come to power under Ramsay MacDonald in 1929, decided to hold a series of Round Table Conferences in London. The first Round Table Conference convened from 12 November 1930 to 19 January 1931. The second Round Table Conference was held in London from 7 September 1931 to 1 December 1931 with the participation of Gandhiji and the Indian National Congress.

This was a speech that was delivered at the plenary session of the Round Table Conference in London on 30 November 1931.

(30 November 1931)

It will be, after all and at best, a paper solution. But immediately you withdraw that wedge, the domestic ties, the domestic affection, the knowledge of common birth—do you suppose that all these will count for nothing?

Were Hindus and Mussalmans and Sikhs always at war with one another when there was no British rule, when there was no English face seen there? We have chapter and verse given to us by Hindu historians and by Mussalman historians to say that we were living in comparative peace even then. And Hindus and Mussalmans in the villages are not—even today—quarrelling. In those days, they were not known to quarrel at all. The late Maulana Muhammad Ali often used to tell me, and he was himself a bit of a historian. He said: 'If God'—'Allah' as he called out—'gives me life, I propose to write the history of Mussalman rule in India; and then I will show, through documents that British people have preserved, that Aurangzeb was not so vile as he has been painted by the British historian; that the Mogul rule was not so bad as it has been shown to us in British history; and so on.' And so have Hindu historians written. This quarrel is not old; this quarrel is coeval with this acute shame. I dare to say, it is coeval with the British advent, and immediately this relationship, the unfortunate, artificial, unnatural relationship between Great Britain and India is transformed into a natural relationship, when it becomes, if it does become, a voluntary partnership to be given up, to be dissolved at the will of either party, when it becomes that, you will find that Hindus, Mussalmans, Sikhs, Europeans, Anglo-Indians, Christians, Untouchables, will all live together as one man.

I do not intend to say much tonight about the princes, but I should be wronging them and should be wronging the Congress if I did not register my claim, not with the Round Table Conference, but with the princes. It is open to the princes to give their terms on which they will join the federation. I have appealed to them to make the path easy for those who inhabit the other part of India, and therefore, I can only make these suggestions for their favourable consideration, for their earnest consideration. I think that if they accepted, no matter what they are, but some fundamental rights as the common property of all India, and if they accepted that position and allowed those rights to be tested by the court, which will be again of their own creation, and if they introduced elements—only elements—of representation on behalf of their subject, I think that they would have gone a long way to conciliate their subjects. They would have gone a long way to show to the world and to show to the whole of India that they are also fired with a democratic spirit, that they do not want to remain undiluted autocrats, but that they want to become constitutional monarch, even as King George of Great Britain is.

An Autonomous Frontier Province: Let India get what she is entitled to and what she can really take, but whatever she gets, and whenever she gets it, let the Frontier Province get complete autonomy today. That frontier will then be a standing demonstration to the whole of India, and therefore, the whole vote of the Congress will be given in favour of the Frontier Province getting provincial autonomy tomorrow. Prime Minister, if you can possibly get your Cabinet to endorse the proposition that from tomorrow the Frontier Province becomes a full-fledged autonomous province, I shall then have a proper footing amongst the frontier tribes and convince them to my assistance when those over the border cast an evil eye on India.

Thanks: Last of all, my last is pleasant task for me. This is perhaps the last time that I shall be sitting with you at negotiations. It is not that I want that. I want to sit at the same table with you in your closets and to negotiate and to plead with you and to go down on bended knees before I take the final lead and final plunge.

But whether I have the good fortune to continue to tender, my cooperation or not does not depend upon me. It largely depends upon you. It depends upon so many circumstances over which neither you nor we may have any control whatsoever. Then, let me perform this pleasant task of giving my thanks to all—from Their Majesties down to the poorest men in the East End where I have taken up my habitation.

In that settlement which represents the poor people of the East End of London, I have become one of them. They have accepted me as a member, and as a favoured member of their family. It will be one of the richest treasures that I shall carry with me. Here, too, I have found nothing but courtesy and nothing but a genuine affection from all with whom I have come in touch. I have come in touch with so many Englishmen. It has been a priceless privilege to me. They have listened to what must have often appeared to them to be unpleasant, although it was true. Although I have often been obliged to say these things to them, they have never shown the slightest impatience or irritation. It is impossible for me to forget these things. No matter what befalls me, no matter what the fortunes may be of this Round Table Conference, one thing I shall certainly carry with me, that is, that from high to low I have found nothing but the utmost courtesy and that utmost affection. I consider that it was well worth my paying this visit to England in order to find this human affection.

It has enhanced, it has deepened, my irrepressible faith in human nature that although Englishmen and English women have been fed upon lies that I see so often disfiguring your press, that although in Lancashire, the Lancashire people had perhaps some reason for becoming irritated against me, I found no irritation and no resentment, even in the operatives. The operatives, men and women, hugged me. They treated me as one of their own. I shall never forget that.

I am carrying with me thousands upon thousands of English friendship. I do not know them, but I read that affection in their eyes as early in the morning I walk through your streets. All this hospitality, all this kindness will never be effaced from my memory, no matter what befalls my unhappy land. I thank you for your forbearance. (Concluded)

6

The Quit India Speeches, 1942

I. *Gandhiji addressed the All India Congress Committee (AICC) at Bombay on 8 August 1942 wherein he declared his plan of action.*

(8 August 1942)

Before you discuss the resolution, let me place before you one or two things. I want you to understand two things very clearly and to consider them from the same point of view from which I am placing them before you. I ask you to consider it from my point of view, because if you approve of it, you will be enjoined to carry out all I say. It will be a great responsibility. There are people who ask me whether I am the same man that I was in 1920, or whether there has been any change in me. You are right in asking that question.

Let me, however, hasten to assure that I am the same Gandhi as I was in 1920. I have not changed in any fundamental respect. I attach the same importance to non-violence that I did then. If at all, my emphasis on it has grown stronger. There is no real contradiction between the present resolution and my previous writings and utterances.

Occasions like the present do not occur in everybody's and but rarely in anybody's life. I want you to know and feel that there is nothing but purest ahimsa in all that I am saying and doing today. The draft resolution of the Working Committee is based on ahimsa, the contemplated struggle similarly has its roots in ahimsa. If, therefore, there is any among you who has lost faith in ahimsa or is wearied of it, let him not vote for this resolution.

Let me explain my position clearly. God has vouchsafed to me a priceless gift in the weapon of ahimsa. I and my ahimsa are on our trail today. If in the present crisis, when the earth is being scorched by the flames of himsa and crying for deliverance, I failed to make use of the God-given talent. God will not forgive me and I shall be judged unwrongly of the great gift. I must act now. I may not hesitate and merely look on, when Russia and China are threatened.

Ours is not a drive for power, but purely a non-violent fight for India's independence. In a violent struggle, a successful general has been often known to affect a military coup and to set up a dictatorship. But under the Congress scheme of things, essentially non-violent as it is, there can be no room for dictatorship. A non-violent soldier of freedom will covet nothing for himself; he fights only for the freedom of his country. The Congress is unconcerned as to who will rule, when freedom is attained. The power, when it comes, will belong to the people of India, and it will be for them to decide to whom it placed in the entrusted. Maybe that the reins will be placed in the hands of the Parsis, for instance—as I would love to see happen—or they may be handed to some others whose names are not heard in the Congress today. It will not be for you then to object saying, 'This community is microscopic. That party did not play its due part in the freedom's struggle; why should it have all the power?' Ever since its inception, the Congress has kept itself meticulously free of the communal taint. It has thought always in terms of the whole nation and has acted accordingly... I know how imperfect our ahimsa is and how far away we are still from the ideal, but in ahimsa, there is no final failure or defeat. I have faith, therefore, that if, in spite of our shortcomings, the big thing does happen, it will be because God wanted to help us by crowning with success our silent, unremitting sadhana for the last twenty-two years.

I believe that in the history of the world, there has not been a more genuinely democratic struggle for freedom than ours. I read Carlyle's *French Revolution* while I was in prison, and Pandit Jawaharlal has told me something about the Russian Revolution. But it is my conviction that inasmuch as these struggles were fought with the weapon of violence, they failed to realize the democratic ideal. In the democracy which I have envisaged, a democracy established by non-violence, there will be equal freedom for all. Everybody will be his own master. It is to join a struggle for such democracy that I invite you today. Once you realize this, you will forget the differences between the Hindus and the Muslims, and think of yourselves as Indians only, engaged in the common struggle for Independence.

Then, there is the question of your attitude towards the British. I have noticed that there is hatred towards the British among the people. The people say they are disgusted with their behaviour. The people make no distinction between British imperialism and the British people. To them, the two are one. This hatred would even make them welcome the Japanese. It is most dangerous. It means that they will exchange one slavery for another. We must get rid of this feeling. Our quarrel is not with the British people, we fight their imperialism. The proposal for the withdrawal of British power did not come out of anger. It came to enable India to play its due part at the present critical juncture. It is not a happy position for a big country like India to be merely helping with money and material obtained willy-nilly from her while the United Nations are conducting the war. We cannot evoke the true spirit of sacrifice and valour, so long as we are not free. I know the British government will not be able to withhold freedom from us, when we have made enough self-sacrifice. We must, therefore, purge ourselves of hatred. Speaking for myself, I can say that I have never felt any hatred. As a matter of fact, I feel myself to be a greater friend of the British—now than ever before. One reason is that they are today in distress. My very friendship, therefore, demands that I should try to save them from their mistakes. As I view the situation, they are on the brink of an abyss. It, therefore, becomes my duty to warn them of their danger, even though it may, for the time being, anger them to the point of cutting off the friendly hand that is stretched out to help them. People may laugh, nevertheless that is my claim. At a time when I may have to launch the biggest struggle of my life, I may not harbor hatred against anybody.

◆

II. *Gandhiji's address before the A.I.C.C. at Bombay on 8 August 1942 delivered in Hindustani.*

I congratulate you on the resolution that you have just passed. I also congratulate the three comrades on the courage they have shown in pressing their amendments to a division, even though they knew that there was an overwhelming majority in favour of the resolution, and I congratulate the thirteen friends who voted against the resolution. In doing so, they had nothing to be ashamed of. For the last twenty years, we have tried to learn not to lose courage, even when we are in a hopeless minority and are laughed at. We have learned to hold on to our beliefs in the confidence that we are in the right. It behaves us to cultivate this courage of conviction, for it ennobles man and raises his moral stature.

I was, therefore, glad to see that these friends had imbibed the principle which I have tried to follow for the last fifty years and more.

Having congratulated them on their courage, let me say that what they asked this committee to accept through their amendments was not the correct representation of the situation. These friends ought to have pondered over the appeal made to them by the Maulana to withdraw their amendments; they should have carefully followed the explanations given by Jawaharlal. Had they done so, it would have been clear to them that the right which they now want the Congress to concede has already been conceded by the Congress.

Time was when every Mussalman claimed the whole of India as his motherland. During the years that the Ali brothers were with me, the assumption underlying all their talks and discussions was that India belonged as much to the Mussalmans as to the Hindus. I can testify to the fact that this was their innermost conviction and nor a mask; I lived with them for years. I spent days and nights in their company. And I make bold to say that their utterances were the honest expression of their beliefs. I know there are some who say that I take things too readily at their face value, that I am gullible. I do not think I am such a simpleton, nor am I so gullible as these friends take me to be. But their criticism does not hurt me. I should prefer to be considered gullible rather than deceitful.

What these communist friends proposed through their amendments is nothing new. It has been repeated from thousands of platforms. Thousands of Mussalmans have told me, that if the Hindu-Muslim question was to be solved satisfactorily, it must be done in my lifetime. I should feel flattered at this; but how can I agree to a proposal which does not appeal to my reason? Hindu-Muslim unity is not a new thing. Millions of Hindus and Mussalmans have sought after it. I consciously strove for its achievement from my boyhood. While at school, I made it a point to cultivate the friendship of Muslims and Parsi co-students. I believed even at that tender age that the Hindus in India, if they wished to live in peace and amity with the other communities, should assiduously cultivate the virtue of neighbourliness. It did not matter, I felt, if I made no special effort to cultivate the friendship with Hindus, but I must make friends with at least a few Mussalmans. It was as counsel for a Mussalman merchant that I went to South Africa. I made friends with other Mussalmans there, even with the opponents of my client, and gained a reputation for integrity and good faith. I had among my friends and co-workers Muslims as well as Parsis. I captured their hearts and when I left finally for India, I left them sad and shedding tears of grief at the separation.

In India, too, I continued my efforts and left no stone unturned to achieve that unity. It was my lifelong aspiration for it that made me offer my fullest cooperation to the Mussalmans in the Khilafat movement. Muslims throughout the country accepted me as their true friend.

How then is it that I have now come to be regarded as so evil and detestable? Had I any axe to grind in supporting the Khilafat movement? True, I did in my heart of hearts cherish a hope that it might enable me to save the cow. I am a worshipper of the cow. I believe the cow and myself to be the creation of the same God, and I am prepared to sacrifice my life in order to save the cow. But, whatever my philosophy of life and my ultimate hopes, I joined the movement in no spirit of bargain. I cooperated in the struggle for the Khilafat solely on order to discharge my obligation to my neighbour who, I saw, was in distress. The Ali brothers, had they been alive today, would have testified to the truth of this assertion. And so would many others bear me out in that it was not a bargain on my part for saving the cow. The cow, like the Khilafat, stood on her own merits. As an honest man, a true neighbour and a faithful friend, it was incumbent on me to stand by the Mussalmans in the hour of their trial.

In those days, I shocked the Hindus by dinning with the Mussalmans, though with the passage of time, they have now got used to it. Maulana Bari told me, however, that though he would not allow me to dine with him, lest someday he should be accused of a sinister motive. And so, whenever I had an occasion to stay with him, he called a Brahmana cook and made social arrangements for separate cooking. Firangi Mahal, his residence, was an old-styled structure with limited accommodation; yet he cheerfully bore all hardships and carried out his resolve from which I could not dislodge him. It was the spirit of courtesy, dignity and nobility that inspired us in those days. They respected one another's religious feelings, and considered it a privilege to do so. Not a trace of suspicion lurked in anybody's heart. Where has all that dignity, that nobility of spirit, disappeared now? I should ask all Mussalmans, including Quaid-i-Azam Jinnah, to recall those glorious days and to find out what has brought us to the present impasse. Quaid-i-Azam Jinnah himself was at one time a Congressman. If today the Congress has incurred his wrath, it is because the canker of suspicion has entered his heart. May God bless him with long life, but when I am gone, he will realize and admit that I had no designs on Mussalmans and that I had never betrayed their interests. Where is the escape for me, if I injure their cause or betray their interests? My life is entirely at their disposal. They are free to put an end to it, whenever they wish to do so. Assaults have been made on my life in the past, but God has spared me till now, and the assailants have repented for their action. But if someone were to shoot me in the belief that he was getting rid of a rascal, he would kill not the real Gandhi, but the one that appeared to him a rascal.

To those who have been indulging in a campaign of an abuse and vilification, I would say, Islam enjoins you not to revile even an enemy. The Prophet treated even enemies with kindness and tried to win them over by his fairness and generosity. Are you followers of that Islam or of any other? If you are followers of the true Islam, does it behave you to distrust the words of one who makes a public declaration of his faith? You may take it from me that one day, you will regret the fact that you distrusted and killed one who was a true and devoted friend of yours. It cuts me to the quick to see that the more I appeal and the more the Maulana importunes, the more intense does the campaign of vilification grow. To me, these abuses are like bullets. They can kill me, even as a bullet can put an end to my life. You may kill me. That will not hurt me. But what of those who indulge in abusing? They bring discredit to Islam. For the fair name of Islam, I appeal to you to resist this unceasing campaign of abuse and vilification.

Maulana saheb is being made a target for the filthiest abuse. Why? Because he refuses to exert on me the pressure of his friendship. He realizes that it is a misuse of friendship to seek up to compel a friend to accept as truth what he knows is an untruth.

To the Quaid-i-Azam, I would say: Whatever is true and valid in the claim for Pakistan is already in your hands. What is wrong and untenable is in nobody's gift, so that it can be made over to you. Even if someone were to succeed in imposing an untruth on others, he would not be able to enjoy for long the fruits of such a coercion. God dislikes pride and keeps away from it. God would not tolerate a forcible imposition of an untruth.

The Quaid-i-Azam says that he is compelled to say bitter things, but that he cannot help giving expression to his thoughts and his feelings. Similarly I would say: I consider myself a friend of Mussalmans. Why should I then not give expression to the things nearest to my heart, even at the cost of displeasing them? How can I conceal my innermost thoughts from them? I should congratulate the Quaid-i-Azam on his frankness in giving expression to his thoughts and feelings, even if they sound bitter to his hearers. But even so, why should the Mussalmans sitting here be reviled, if they do not see eye to eye with him? If millions of Mussalmans are with you, can you afford to ignore the handful of Mussalmans who may appear to you to be misguided? Why should one with the following of several millions be afraid of a majority community, or of the minority being swamped by the majority? How did the Prophet work among the Arabs and the Mussalmans? How did he propagate Islam? Did he say he would propagate Islam only when he commanded a majority? I appeal to you for the sake of Islam to ponder over what I say. There is neither fair play nor justice in saying that the Congress must accept a thing, even if it does not believe in it and even if it goes counter to principles it holds dear.

Rajaji said: 'I do not believe in Pakistan. But Mussalmans ask for it, Mr Jinnah asks for it, and it has become an obsession with them. Why not then say, "yes" to them just now? The same Mr Jinnah will later on realize the disadvantages of Pakistan and will forgo the demand.' I said: 'It is not fair to accept as true a thing which I hold to be untrue, and ask others to do say in the belief that the demand will not be pressed when the time comes for settling in finally. If I hold the demand to be just, I should concede it this very day. I should not agree to it merely in order to placate Jinnah saheb. Many friends have come and asked me to agree to it for the time being to placate Mr Jinnah, disarm his suspicious and to see how he reacts to it. But I cannot be party to a course of action with a false promise. At any rate, it is not my method.'

The Congress has no sanction but the moral one for enforcing its decisions. It believes that true democracy can only be the outcome of non-violence. The structure of a world federation can be raised only on a foundation of non-violence, and violence will have to be totally abjured from world affairs. If this is true, the solution of Hindu-Muslim question, too, cannot be achieved by a resort to violence. If the Hindus tyrannize over the Mussalmans, with what face will they talk of a world federation? It is for the same reason that I do not believe in the possibility of establishing world peace through violence as the English and American statesmen propose to do. The Congress has agreed to submit all the differences to an impartial international tribunal and to abide by its decisions. If even this fairest of proposals is unacceptable, the only course that remains open is that of the sword, of violence. How can I persuade myself to agree to impossibility? To demand the vivisection of a living organism is to ask for its very life. It is a call to war. The Congress cannot be party to such a fratricidal war. Those Hindus who, like Dr Moonje and Shri Savarkar, believe in the doctrine of the sword may seek to keep the Mussalmans under Hindus' domination. I do not represent that section. I represent the Congress. You want to kill the Congress which is the goose that lays golden eggs. If you distrust the Congress, you may rest assured that there is to be perpetual war between the Hindus and the Mussalmans, and the country will be doomed to continue warfare and bloodshed. If such warfare is to be our lot, I shall not live to witness it.

It is for that reason that I say to Jinnah saheb, 'You may take it from me that whatever in your demand for Pakistan accords with considerations of justice and equity is lying in your pocket; whatever in the demand is contrary to justice and equity, you can take only by the sword and in no other manner.'

There is much in my heart that I would like to pour out before this assembly. One thing which was uppermost in my heart I have already dealt with. You may take it from me that it is with me a matter of life and death. If we Hindus and Mussalmans mean to achieve a heart unity, without the slightest mental reservation on the part of either, we must first unite in the effort to be free from the shackles of this empire.

If Pakistan after all is to be a portion of India, what objection can there be for Mussalmans against joining this struggle for India's freedom? The Hindus and Mussalmans must, therefore, unite in the first instance on the issue of fighting for freedom. Jinnah saheb thinks the war will last long. I do not agree with him. If the war goes on for six months more, how shall we able to save China?

I, therefore, want freedom immediately, this very night, before dawn, if it can be had. Freedom cannot now wait for the realization of communal unity. If that unity is not achieved, sacrifices necessary for it will have to be much greater than would have otherwise sufficed. But the Congress must win freedom or be wiped out in the effort. And forget not that the freedom which the Congress is struggling to achieve will not be for the Congressmen alone but for all the forty crores of the Indian people. Congressmen must forever remain humble servants of the people.

The Quaid-i-Azam has said that the Muslim League is prepared to take over the rule from the Britishers if they are prepared to hand it over to the Muslim League, for the British took over the empire from the hands of the Muslims. This, however, will be Muslim Raj. The offer made by Maulana saheb and by me does not imply establishment of Muslim Raj or Muslim domination. The Congress does not believe in the domination of any group or any community. It believes in democracy which includes in its orbit Muslims, Hindus, Christians, Parsis, Jews—every one of the communities inhabiting this vast country. If Muslim Raj is inevitable, then let it be; but how can we give it the stamp of our assent? How can we agree to the domination of one community over the others?

Millions of Mussalmans in this country come from Hindu stock. How can their homeland be any other than India? My eldest son embraced Islam some years back. What would his homeland be—Porbandar or the Punjab? I ask the Mussalmans: 'If India is not your homeland, what other country do you belong to? In what separate homeland would you put my son who embraced Islam?' His mother wrote him a letter after his conversion, asking him if he had on embracing Islam given up drinking which Islam forbids to its follower. To those who gloated over the conversion, she wrote to say: 'I do not mind his becoming a Mussalman, so much as his drinking. Will you, as pious Mussalmans, tolerate his drinking even after his conversion? He has reduced himself to the state of a rake by drinking. If you are going to make a man of him again, his conversion will have been turned to good account. You will, therefore, please see that he as a Mussalman abjures wine and woman. If that change does not come about, his conversion goes in vain and our non-cooperation with him will have to continue.'

India is, without doubt, the homeland of all the Mussalmans inhabiting this country. Every Mussalman should therefore co-operate in the fight for India's freedom. The Congress does not belong to any one class or community; it belongs to the whole nation. It is open to Mussalmans to take possession of the Congress. They can, if they like, swamp the Congress by their numbers, and can steer it along the course which appeals to them. The Congress is fighting not on behalf of the Hindu but on behalf of the whole nation, including the minorities. It would hurt me to hear of a single instance of a Mussalman being killed by a Congressman. In the coming revolution, Congressmen will sacrifice their lives in order to protect the Mussalman against a Hindu's attack and vice versa. It is a part of their creed, and is one of the essentials of non-violence. You will be excepted on occasions like these not to lose your heads. Every Congressman, whether a Hindu or a Mussalman, owes this duty to the organization to which he belongs. The Mussalman who will act in this manner will render a service to Islam. Mutual trust is essential for success in the final nation-wide struggle that is to come.

I have said that much greater sacrifice will have to be made this time in the wake of our struggle because of the opposition from the Muslim League and from Englishmen. You have seen the secret circular issued by Sir Frederick Puckle. It is a suicidal course that he has taken. It contains an open incitement to organizations which crop up like mushrooms to combine to fight the Congress. We have thus to deal with an empire whose ways are crooked. Ours is a straight path which we can tread even with our eyes closed. That is the beauty of satyagraha.

In satyagraha, there is no place for fraud or falsehood, or any kind of untruth. Fraud and untruth today are stalking the world. I cannot be a helpless witness to such a situation. I have traveled all over India as perhaps nobody in the present age has. The voiceless millions of the land saw in me their friend and representative, and I identified myself with them to an extent it was possible for a human being to do. I saw trust in their eyes, which I now want to turn to good account in fighting this empire upheld on untruth and violence. However gigantic the preparations that the empire has made, we must get out of its clutches. How can I remain silent at this supreme hour and hide my light under the bushel? Shall I ask the Japanese to tarry awhile? If today I sit quiet and inactive, God will take me to task for not using up the treasure He had given me, in the midst of the conflagration that is enveloping the whole world. Had the condition been different, I should have asked you to wait yet awhile. But the situation now has become intolerable, and the Congress has no other course left for it.

Nevertheless, the actual struggle does not commence this moment. You have only placed all your powers in my hands. I will now wait upon the viceroy and plead with him for the acceptance of the Congress demand. That process is likely to take two or three weeks. What would you do in the meanwhile? What is the programme, for the interval, in which all can participate? As you know, the spinning wheel is the first thing that occurs to me. I made the same answer to the Maulana. He would have none of it, though he understood its import later. The fourteen-fold constructive programme is, of course, there for you to carry out. What more should you do? I will tell you. Every one of you should, from this moment onwards, consider yourself a free man or woman, and act as if you are free and are no longer under the heel of this imperialism.

It is not a make-believe that I am suggesting to you. It is the very essence of freedom. The bond of the slave is snapped the moment he considers himself to be a free being. He will plainly tell the master: 'I was your bond slave till this moment, but I am a slave no longer. You may kill me if you like, but if you keep me alive, I wish to tell you that if you release me from the bondage, of your own accord, I will ask for nothing more from you. You used to feed and clothe me, though I could have provided food and clothing for myself by my labour. I hitherto depended on you instead of on God, for food and raiment. But God has now inspired me with an urge for freedom and I am today a free man, and will no longer depend on you.'

You may take it from me that I am not going to strike a bargain with the viceroy for ministries and the like. I am not going to be satisfied with anything short of complete freedom. Maybe he will propose the abolition of salt tax, the drink evil, etc. But I will say, 'Nothing less than freedom.'

Here is a mantra, a short one, that I give you. You may imprint it on your hearts and let every breath of yours give expression to it. The mantra is: 'Do or Die.' We shall either free India or die in the attempt; we shall not live to see the perpetuation of our slavery. Every true Congressman or woman will join the struggle with an inflexible determination not to remain alive to see the country in bondage and slavery. Let that be your pledge. Keep jails out of your consideration. If the government keeps me free, I will not put on the government the strain of maintaining a large number of prisoners at a time, when it is in trouble. Let every man and woman live every moment of his or her life hereafter in the consciousness that he or she eats or lives for achieving freedom and will die, if need be, to attain that goal. Take a pledge, with God and your own conscience as witness, that you will no longer rest till freedom is achieved and will be prepared to lay down your lives in the attempt to achieve it. He who loses his life will gain it; he who will seek to save it shall lose it. Freedom is not for the coward or the faint-hearted. A word to the journalists. I congratulate you on the support you have hitherto given to the national demand. I know the restrictions and handicaps under which you have to labour. But I would now ask you to snap the chains that bind you. It should be the proud privilege of the newspapers to lead and set an example in laying down one's life for freedom.

You have the pen which the government can't suppress. I know you have large properties in the form of printing presses, etc., and you would be afraid lest the government should attach them. I do not ask you to invite an attachment of the printing-press voluntarily. For myself, I would not suppress my pen, even if the press was to be attached. As you know my press was attached in the past and returned later on. But I do not ask from you that final sacrifice. I suggest a middle way. You should now wind up your standing committee, and you may declare that you will give up the pen only when India has won her freedom. You may tell Sir Frederick Puckle that he can't except from you a command performance, that his press notes are full of untruth, and that you will refuse to publish them. You will openly declare that you are wholeheartedly with the Congress. If you do this, you will have changed the atmosphere before the fight actually begins.

From the princes, I ask, with all respect due to them, a very small thing. I am a well-wisher of the princes. I was born in a state. My grandfather refused to salute with his right hand any prince other than his own. But he did not say to the prince, as I fell he ought to have said, that even his own master could not compel him, his minister, to act against his conscience. I have eaten the prince's salt and I would not be false to it. As a faithful servant, it is my duty to warn the princes that if they will act while I am still alive, the princes may come to occupy an honourable place in free India. In Jawaharlal's scheme of free India, no privileges or the privileged classes have a place. Jawaharlal considers all property to be state owned. He wants planned economy. He wants to reconstruct India according to plan. He likes to fly; I do not. I have kept a place for the princes and the zamindars in India that I envisage. I would ask the princes in all humility to enjoy through renunciation. The princes may renounce ownership over their properties and become their trustees in the true sense of the term. I visualize God in the assemblage of people. The princes may say to their people: 'You are the owners and masters of the state and we are your servants.' I would ask the princes to become servants of the people and render to them an account of their own services. The empire too bestows power on the princes, but they should prefer to derive power from their own people; and if they want to indulge in some innocent pleasures, they may seek to do so as servants of the people. I do not want the princes to live as paupers. But I would ask them: 'Do you want to remain slaves for all time? Why should you, instead of paying homage to a foreign power, not accept the sovereignty of your own people?' You may write to the political department: 'The people are now awake. How are we to withstand an avalanche before which even the large empires are crumbling? We, therefore, shall belong to the people from today onwards. We shall sink or swim with them.' Believe me, there is nothing unconstitutional in the course I am suggesting. There are, so far as I know, no treaties enabling the empire to coerce the princes. The people of the states will also declare that though they are the princes' subjects, they are part of the Indian nation and that they will accept the leadership of the princes, if the latter cast their lot with the people, the latter will meet death bravely and unflinchingly, but will not go back on their word.

Nothing, however, should be done secretly. This is an open rebellion. In this struggle, secrecy is a sin. A free man would not engage in a secret movement. It is likely that when you gain freedom, you will have a C.I.D. of your own, in spite of my advice to the contrary. But in the present struggle, we have to work openly and to receive bullets on our chest, without taking to heels.

I have a word to say to the government servants also. They may not, if they like, resign their posts yet. The late Justice Ranade did not resign his post, but he openly declared that he belonged to the Congress. He said to the government that though he was a judge, he was a Congressman and would openly attend the sessions of the Congress, but that at the same time, he would not let his political views warp his impartiality on the bench. He held Social Reform Conference in the very pandal of the Congress. I would ask all the government servants to follow in the footsteps of Ranade and to declare their allegiance to the Congress as an answer to the secret circular issued by Sir Frederick Puckle.

This is all that I ask of you just now. I will now write to the viceroy. You will be able to read the correspondence not just now but when I publish it with the viceroy's consent. But you are free to aver that you support the demand to be put forth in my letter. A judge came to me and said: 'We get secret circulars from high quarters. What are we to do?' I replied, 'If I were in your place, I would ignore the circulars. You may openly say to the government: "I have received your secret circular. I am, however, with the Congress. Though I serve the government for my livelihood, I am not going to obey these secret circulars or to employ underhand methods".'

Soldiers too are covered by the present programme. I do not ask them just now to resign their posts and to leave the army. The soldiers come to me, Jawaharlal and the

Maulana, and say: 'We are wholly with you. We are tired of the governmental tyranny.' To these soldiers, I would say: 'You may say to the government: "Our hearts are with the Congress. We are not going to leave our posts. We will serve you so long as we receive your salaries. We will obey your just orders, but will refuse to fire on our own people".'

To those who lack the courage to do this much, I have nothing to say. They will go their own way. But if you can do this much, you may take it from me that the whole atmosphere will be electrified. Let the government then shower bombs, if they like. But no power on earth will then be able to keep you in bondage any longer.

If the students want to join the struggle only to go back to their studies after a while, I would not invite them to it. For the present, however, till the time that I frame a programme for the struggle, I would ask the students to say to their professors: 'We belong to the Congress. Do you belong to the Congress, or to the government? If you belong to the Congress, you need not vacate your posts. You will remain at your posts, but teach us and lead us unto freedom.' In all fights for freedom, the world over, the students have made very large contributions.

If in the interval that is left to us before the actual fight begins, if you do even the little I have suggested to you, you will have changed the atmosphere and will have prepared the ground for the next step.

There is much I should like to say. But my heart is heavy. I have already taken up much of your time. I have yet to say a few words in English also. I thank you for the patience and attention with which you have listened to me, even at this late hour. It is just what true soldiers would do. For the last twenty-two years, I have controlled my speech and pen and have stored up my energy. He is a true brahmachari who does not fritter away his energy. He will, therefore, always control his speech. That has been my conscious effort all these years. But today the occasion has come when I have to unburden my heart before you. I have done so, even though it meant putting a strain on your patience; and I do not regret having done it. I have given you my message and through you I have delivered it to the whole of India.

◆

III. *The following is the concluding portion of Gandhiji's speech before the A.I.C.C. at Bombay on 8 August 1942.*

I have taken such an inordinately long time over pouring out what was agitating my soul, to those whom I had just now the privilege of serving. I have been called their leader or, in the military language, their commander. But I do not look at my position in that light. I have no weapon but love to wield my authority over any one. I do sport a stick which you can break into bits without the slightest exertion. It is simply my staff with the help of which I walk. Such a cripple is not elated, when he has been called upon to bear the greatest burden. You can share that burden only when I appear before you not as your commander but as a humble servant. And he who serves best is the chief among equals.

Therefore, I was bound to share with you such thoughts as were welling up in my breast and tell you, in as summary a manner as I can, what I expect you to do as the first step.

Let me tell you at the outset that the real struggle does not commence today. I have yet to go through much ceremonial as I always do. The burden, I confess, would be almost unbearable. I have to continue to reason in those circles with whom I have lost my credit and who have no trust left in me. I know that in the course of the last few weeks, I have forfeited my credit with a large number of friends, so much so, that they have begun to doubt not only my wisdom but even my honesty. Now I hold my wisdom is not such a treasure which I cannot afford to lose; but my honesty is a precious treasure to me and I can ill-afford to lose it. I seem, however, to have lost it for the time being.

Friend of the empire

Such occasions arise in the life of the man who is a pure seeker after truth and who would seek to serve the humanity and his country to the best of his lights without fear or hypocrisy. For the last fifty years, I have known no other way. I have been a humble servant of humanity and have rendered on more than one occasion such services as I could to the Empire, and here let me say without fear of challenge that throughout my career never have I asked for any personal favour. I have enjoyed the privilege of friendship as I enjoy it today with Lord Linlithgow. It is a friendship which has outgrown official relationship. Whether Lord Linlithgow will bear me out, I do not know, but there is a personal bond between him and myself. He once introduced me to his daughter. His son-in-law, the A.D.C. was drawn towards me. He fell in love with Mahadev more than with me and Lady Anna and he came to me. She is an obedient and favourite daughter. I take interest in their welfare. I take the liberty to give out these personal and sacred tit-bits only to give you an earnest of the personal bond which exists between us; and yet let me declare here that that personal bond will never interfere with the stubborn struggle on which, if it falls to my lot, I may have to launch against Lord Linlithgow, as the representative of the Empire. I will have to resist the might of that Empire with the might of the dumb millions with no limit but of non-violence as policy confined to this struggle. It is a terrible job to have to offer resistance to a viceroy with whom I enjoy such relations. He has more than once trusted my word, often about my people. I would love to repeat that experiment, as it stands to his credit. I mention this with great pride and pleasure. I mention it as an earnest of my desire to be true to the Empire when that Empire forfeited my trust and the Englishman who was its viceroy came to know it.

Charlie Andrews

Then there is the sacred memory of Charlie Andrews which wells up within me. At this moment, the spirit of Andrews hovers about me. For me, he sums up the brightest traditions of English culture. I enjoyed closer relations with him than with most Indians. I enjoyed his confidence. There were no secrets between us. We exchanged our hearts every day. Whatever was in his heart, he would blurt out without the slightest hesitation or reservation. It is true he was a friend of Gurudev, but he looked upon Gurudev with awe. He had that peculiar humility. But with me, he became the closest friend. Years ago, he came to me with a note of introduction from Gokhale. Pearson and he were the first-rank specimens of Englishmen. I know that his spirit is listening to me.

Then I have got a warm letter of congratulations from

the Metropolitan of Calcutta. I hold him to be a man of God. Today he is opposed to me.

Voice of conscience

With all this background, I want to declare to the world, although I may have forfeited the regard of many friends in the West and I must bow my head low; but even for their friendship or love, I must not suppress the voice of conscience—promoting of my inner basic nature today. There is something within me impelling me to cry out my agony. I have known humanity. I have studied something of Psychology. Such a man knows exactly what it is. I do not mind how you describe it. That voice within tells me, 'You have to stand against the whole world, although you may have to stand alone. You have to stare in the face of the whole world, although the world may look at you with bloodshot eyes. Do not fear. Trust the little voice residing within your heart. It says: "Forsake friends, wife and all; but testify to that for which you have lived and for which you have to die."' I want to live my full span of life. And for me, I put my span of life at 120 years. By that time India will be free, the world will be free.

Real freedom

Let me tell you that I do not regard England or for that matter America as free countries. They are free after their own fashion, free to hold in bondage coloured races of the earth. Are England and America fighting for the liberty of these races today? If not, do not ask me to wait until after the war.

You shall not limit my concept of freedom. The English and American teachers, their history, their magnificent poetry have not said that you shall not broaden the interpretation of freedom. And according to my interpretation of that freedom, I am constrained to say they are strangers to that freedom which their teachers and poets have described. If they will know the real freedom, they should come to India. They have to come not with pride or arrogance, but in the spite of real earnest seekers of truth. It is a fundamental truth which India has been experimenting with for twenty-two years.

Congress and non-violence

Unconsciously from its very foundations long ago, the Congress has been building on non-violence known as constitutional methods. Dadabhai and Pherozeshah, who had held the Congress India in the palm of their hands, became rebels. They were lovers of the Congress. They were its masters. But above all they were real servants. They never countenanced murder, secrecy and the like. I confess there are many black sheep amongst us Congressmen. But I trust the whole of India today to launch upon a non-violent struggle. I trust because of my nature to rely upon the innate goodness of human nature, which perceives the truth and prevails during crisis, as if by instinct. But even if I am deceived in this, I shall not swerve. I shall not flinch. From its very inception, the Congress based its policy on peaceful methods, included swaraj and the subsequent generations added non-violence. When Dadabhai entered the British Parliament, Salisbury dubbed him as a black man; but the English people defeated Salisbury and Dadabhai went to the

Parliament by their vote. India was delirious with joy. These things, however, India has outgrown.

I will go ahead

It is, however, with all these things as the background that I want Englishmen, Europeans and all the United Nations to examine in their hearts what crime had India committed in demanding Independence. I ask, is it right for you to distrust such an organization with all its background, tradition and record of over half a century and misrepresent its endeavours before all the world by every means at your command? Is it right that by hook or by crook, aided by the foreign press, aided by the president of the U.S.A., or even by the generalissimo of China who has yet to win his laurels, you should present India's struggle in shocking caricature? I have met the generalissimo. I have known him through Madame Shek who was my interpreter; and though he seemed inscrutable to me, not so Madame Shek; and he allowed me to read his mind through her.

There is a chorus of disapproval and righteous protest all over the world against us. They say we are erring, the move is inopportune. I had great regard for British diplomacy which has enabled them to hold the Empire so long. Now it stinks in my nostrils, and others have studied that diplomacy and are putting it into practice. They may succeed in getting, through these methods, world opinion on their side for a time; but India will speak against that world opinion. She will raise her voice against all the organized propaganda. I will speak against it. Even if all the United Nations opposed me, even if the whole of India forsakes me, I will say, 'You are wrong! India will wrench with non-violence her liberty from unwilling hands.' I will go ahead not for India's sake alone, but for the sake of the world. Even if my eyes close before there is freedom, non-violence will not end. They will be dealing a mortal blow to China and to Russia if they oppose the freedom of non-violent India which is pleading with bended knees for the fulfillment of debt long overdue. Does a creditor ever go to debtor like that? And even when India is met with such angry opposition, she says, 'We won't hit below the belt, we have learnt sufficient gentlemanliness. We are pledged to non-violence.' I have been the author of non-embarrassment policy of the Congress and yet today, you find me talking this strong language. I say it is consistent with our honour. If a man holds me by the neck and wants to drown me, may I not struggle to free myself directly? There is no inconsistency in our position today.

Appeal to the United Nations

There are representatives of the foreign press assembled here today. Through them I wish to say to the world that the United Powers who somehow or other say that they have need for India, have the opportunity now to declare India free and prove their bona fides. If they miss it, they will be missing the opportunity of their lifetime, and history will record that they did not discharge their obligations to India in time, and lost the battle. I want the blessings of the whole world so that I may succeed with them. I do not want the United Powers to go beyond their obvious limitations. I do not want them to accept non-violence and disarm today. There is a fundamental difference between fascism and this imperialism which I am fighting. Do the British get from India which they hold in bondage? Think what difference it would make if India was to participate as a free ally. That freedom, if it is to come, must come today. It will have no taste left in it today if you, who have the power to help, cannot exercise it. If you can exercise it, under the glow of freedom what seems impossible, today, will become possible tomorrow. If India feels that freedom, she will command that freedom for China. The road for running to Russia's help will be open. The Englishmen did not die in Malaya or on Burma soil. What shall enable us to retrieve the situation? Where shall I go, and where shall I take the forty crores of India? How is this vast mass of humanity to be aglow in the cause of world deliverance, unless and until it has touched and felt freedom? Today, they have no touch of life left. It has been crushed out of them. If lustre is to be put into their eyes, freedom has to come not tomorrow, but today.

Do or die

I have pledged the Congress and the Congress will do or die.

7

Speech before Inter-Asian Relations Conference, 1947

This was a momentous occasion at the closing session of the Inter-Asian Relations Conference held on 2 April 1947. Mrs Naidu introduced Mahatma Gandhi as 'one of the greatest Asians of the age' and visitors, delegates and observers gave a great ovation to Gandhiji.

(2 April 1947)

I do not think that I should apologize to you for having to speak in a foreign tongue. I wonder if this loudspeaker carries my voice to the farthest end of this vast audience. If some of those who are far away are unable to listen to what I may say, it will be the fault of the loudspeaker.

I was going to tell you that I do not wish to apologize. I dare not. You cannot understand the provincial language, which is my mother tongue. I do not want to insult you by speaking in my own language (Gujarati). Our national speech is Hindustani. I know that it will be a long time before it can be made into an international speech. For international commerce, undoubtedly, English occupies the first place. I used to hear that French was the language of diplomacy. I was told, when I was young, that if I wanted to go from one end of Europe to the other, I must try to pick up French. I tried to learn French, in order that I may be able to make myself understood. There is a rivalry between the French and the English. Having been taught English, I have naturally to resort to it.

I was wondering, as to what I was to speak to you. I wanted to collect my thoughts, but, let me confess to you that I had no time. Yet I had promised yesterday that I would try to say a few words. While I was coming with Badshah Khan, I asked for a little piece of paper and pencil. I got a pen, instead of a pencil. I tried to scribble a few words. You will be sorry to hear that piece of paper is not by my side, though I remember what I wanted to say.

You, friends, have not seen the real India and you are not meeting in conference in the midst of real India. Delhi, Bombay, Madras, Calcutta, Lahore—all these are big cities and are, therefore, influenced by the West.

I then thought of a story. It was in French and was translated for me by an Anglo-French philosopher. He was an unselfish man. He befriended me without having known me, because he always sided with the minorities. I was not then in my own country. I was not only in a hopeless minority, but in a despised minority, if the Europeans in South Africa will forgive me for saying so. I was a coolie lawyer. At the time, we had no coolie doctors, and we had no coolie lawyers. I was the first in the field. You know, perhaps, what is meant by the word 'coolie'.

This friend—his mother was a French woman and his father was an Englishman—said: 'I want to translate for you a French story. There were three scientists who went out from France in search of truth. They went to different parts of Asia. One of them found his way to India. He began to search. He went to the so-called cities of those times—naturally this was before British occupation, before even the Mogul period. He saw the so-called high-caste people, men and women, till he felt at a loss. Finally, he went to one humble cottage and there he found the truth that he was in search of.'

If you really want to see India's villages at their best, you have to find it in the humble bhangi homes of such villages. There are seven lakhs of such villages, and thirty–eighty crores of people inhabit them.

If some of you see the Indian villages, you will not be fascinated by the sight. You will have to scratch below the dung heap. I do not pretend to say that they were places of paradise. Today, they are really dung heaps. They were not like that before. What I say is not from history, but from what I have seen myself. I have traveled from one end of India to the other, and I have seen the miserable specimens of humanity with the lustreless eyes. They are India. In these humble cottages, in the midst of these dung heaps, are to be found humble Bhangis, in whom you find the concentrated essence of wisdom.

Again, I have learnt from books—books written by English historians. We read books written by English historians, but we do not write in our own mother tongue, or in the national language, Hindustani. We study our history through English books, rather than through originals. That is the cultural conquest which India has undergone.

The first of these wise men was Zoroaster. He belonged to the East. He was followed by Buddha who belonged to the East-India. Who followed Buddha? Jesus, who came from the East. Before Jesus was Moses, who belonged to Palestine, though he was born in Egypt. And after Jesus came Mohamed. I omit my reference to Krishna and Rama and other lights. I do not call them lesser lights, but they are less known to the literary world. All the same, I do not know a single person in the world to match these men to Asia. And then what happened? Christianity became disfigured when it went to the West. I am sorry to have to say that—I would not talk any further.

I have told you the story, in order to make you understand that what you see in the big cities is not the real India. Certainly, the carnage that is going on before our very eyes is a shameful thing. As I said yesterday, do not carry the memory of that carnage beyond the confines of India. What I want you to understand is the message of Asia. It is not to be learnt through the Western spectacles or by imitating the atom bomb. If you want to give a message to the West, it must be the message of love and the message of truth. I do not want merely to appeal to your head. I want to capture your heart.

In this age of democracy, in this age of awakening of the poorest of the poor, you can redeliver this message with the greatest emphasis. You will complete the conquest of the West, not through vengeance, because you have been exploited, but with real understanding. I am sanguine, if all of you put your hearts together—not merely heads—to understand the secret of the message these wise men of the East have left to us, and us if we really become worthy of that great message, the conquest of the West will be completed. This conquest will be loved by the West itself.

The West is today pinning for wisdom. It is despairing of a multiplication of the atom bombs, because the atom bombs mean utter destruction, not merely of the West, but of the whole world, as if the prophecy of the Bible is going to be fulfilled and there is to be a perfect deluge. It is up to you to tell the world of its wickedness and sin—that is the heritage your teachers and my teachers have taught Asia.

8

On Kashmir

This speech was delivered on 4 January 1948 at the prayer meeting.

(4 January 1948)

Today there is talk of war everywhere. Everyone fears a war breaking out between the two countries. If that happens, it will be a calamity both for India and for Pakistan. India has written to the U.N. because whenever there is a fear of conflict anywhere, the U.N. is asked to promote a settlement and to stop fighting from breaking out. India, therefore, wrote to the U.N.O. that however trivial the issue may appear to be, it could lead to a war between the two countries. It is a long memorandum and it has been cabled. Pakistan's leaders Zafrullah Khan and Liaquat Ali Khan have since issued long statements. I would take leave to say that their argument does not appeal to me. You may ask if I approve of the Union Government approaching the U.N.O. I may say that I both approve and do not approve of what they did. I approve of it, because after all what else are they to do? They are convinced that what they are doing is right. If there are raids from outside the frontier of Kashmir, the obvious conclusion is that it must be with the connivance of Pakistan. Pakistan can deny it. But the denial does not settle the matter.

Kashmir has acceded the accession upon certain conditions. If Pakistan harasses Kashmir and if Sheikh Abdullah, who is the leader of Kashmir, asks the Indian Union for help, the latter is bound to send help. Such help, therefore, was sent to Kashmir. At the same time, Pakistan is being requested to get out of Kashmir and to arrive at a settlement with India over the question through bilateral negotiations. If no settlement can be reached in this way, then a war is inevitable. It is to avoid the possibility of war that the Union Government has taken the step it did. Whether they are right in doing so or not, God alone knows. Whatever might have been the attitude of Pakistan, if I had my way, I would have invited Pakistan's representatives to India and we could have met, discussed the matter and worked out some settlement. They keep saying that they want an amicable settlement, but they do nothing to create the conditions for such a settlement. I shall, therefore, humbly say to the responsible leaders of Pakistan that though we are now two countries—which is a thing I never wanted—we should at least try to arrive at an agreement so that we could live as peaceful neighbours. Let us grant for the sake of argument that all Indians are bad, but Pakistan at least is a newborn nation which has more ever come into being in the name of religion and it should at least keep itself clean. But they themselves make no such claim. It is not their argument that Muslims have committed no atrocities in Pakistan. I shall, therefore, suggest that it is now their duty, as far as possible, to arrive at an amicable understanding with India and live in harmony with her. Mistakes were made on both sides. Of this, I have no doubt. But this does not mean that we should persist in those mistakes, for then in the end, we shall only destroy ourselves in a war and the whole of the subcontinent will pass into the hands of some third power. That will be the worst imaginable fate for us. I shudder to think of it. Therefore, the two Dominions should come together with God as witness and find a settlement. The matter is now before the U.N.O. It cannot be withdrawn from there. But if India and Pakistan come to a settlement, the big powers in the U.N.O. will have to endorse that settlement. They will not object to the settlement. They themselves can only say that they will do their best to see that the two countries arrive at an understanding through mutual discussions. Let us pray to God to grant that we may either learn to live in amity with each other or, if we must fight, to let us fight to the very end. That may be folly but sooner or later, it will purify us. Now, a few words about Delhi... I came to know of the incidents which took place last evening through Brijkishan. I had gone to the camp for the evening prayer. I came away after the prayer, but he had stayed over to talk to the people in the camp. There are some Muslim houses at a little distance from the camp. About four or five hundred inmates of the camp—mostly women and children but also some men—issued out of the camp to take possession of the houses. I am told they did not indulge in any kind of violence. Some of the houses were vacant. Some were occupied by the owners. They tried to take possession even of the latter. The police were near at hand. They immediately went to the spot and brought the situation under control at about 9 o'clock according to the information I have. The police have stayed on there. I understand they had to use tear gas. Tear gas does not kill but it can be pretty painful. I am told that something has happened today again.

All I can say is that is a matter of great shame for us. Have not the refugees learnt even from their immense suffering that they have to exercise some restraint? It is highly improper to go and occupy other people's houses. It is for the government to find them shelter or whatever else their need. Today the government is our own. But if we defy our own government and defy the police and forcibly occupy houses, the government is not likely to continue for long. It is still worse that such things should happen in the capital city of India where there are so many ambassadors from all over the world. Do we want to show them the spectacle of people occupying whatever they can? It is all the more regrettable that women and children were used as a shield. It is inhuman. It is like Muslim rulers keeping a herd of cows in the vanguard of their armies to make sure that the Hindus would not fight. It is uncivilized, barbaric behaviour. It is still more barbaric to put women and children in front to provide against the police making a lathi-charge. It is abuse of womanhood. I must humbly ask all the refugees—women and children—not to behave in this way. Let them settle down. If they don't, then apart from a war between India and Pakistan, we may kill ourselves in mutual strife. We may lose Delhi and make ourselves the laughing stock of the world. If we want to keep India a free country, we must stop the things that are going on at present.

9

Speech on the Eve of the Last Fast, 1948

12 January 1948

My fast as a protest

One fasts for health's sake under laws governing health, fasts as a penance for a wrong done and felt as such. In these fasts, the fasting one need not believe in ahimsa. Here is, however, a fast which a votary of non-violence sometimes feels impelled to undertake by way of protest against some wrong done by society, and this he does when as a votary of ahimsa has no other remedy left. Such an occasion has come my way.

When on 9 September, I returned to Delhi from Calcutta, it was to proceed to the West Punjab (Pakistan-occupied Punjab). But that was not to be. Gay Delhi looked a city of the dead. As I alighted from the train, I observed gloom on every face I saw. Even the Sardar, whom humour and the joy that humour gives never desert, was no exception this time. The cause of it I did not know. He was on the platform to receive me. He lost no time in giving me the sad news of the disturbances that had taken place in the Metropolis of the union. At once, I saw that I had to be in Delhi and 'do or die.' There is an apparent calm brought about by prompt military and police action. But there is storm within the breast. It may burst forth any day. This I count as no fulfillment of the vow to 'do,' which alone can keep me from death, the incomparable friend. I yearn for heart friendship between the Hindus, the Sikhs and the Muslims. It subsisted between them the other day. Today, it is non-existent. It is a state that no Indian patriot worthy of the name can contemplate with equanimity. Though the voice within has been beckoning for a long time, I have been shutting my ears to it, lest it may be the voice of Satan, otherwise called my weakness. I never like to feel resourceless; a satyagrahi never should. Fasting is his last resort in the place of the sword—his or others.' I have no answer to return to the Muslim friends who see me from day to day as to what they should do. My impotence has been gnawing at me of late. It will go immediately the fast is undertaken. I have been brooding over it for the last three days. The final conclusion has flashed upon me and it makes me happy. No man, if he is pure, has anything more precious to give than his life. I hope and pray that I have that purity in me to justify the step.

Worthy of blessing

I ask you all to bless the effort and to pray for me and with me. The fast begins from the first meal tomorrow. The period is indefinite and I may drink water with or without salts and sour limes. It will end when and if I am satisfied that there is a reunion of hearts of all the communities brought about without any outside pressure, but from an awakened sense of duty. The reward will be the regaining of India's dwindling prestige and her fast-fading sovereignty over the heart of Asia and there through the world. I flatter myself with belief that the loss of her soul by India will mean the loss of the hope of the aching, storm-tossed and hungry world. Let no friend, or foe if there be one, be angry with me. There are friends who do not believe in the method of the fast for the reclamation of the human mind. They will bear with me and extend to me the same liberty of action that they claim for themselves. With God as my supreme and sole counsellor, I felt that I must take the decision without any other adviser. If I made a mistake and discovered it, I shall have no hesitation in proclaiming it from the housetop and retracing my faulty step. There is clear indication, as I claim there is, of the inner voice, it will not be gainsaid. I plead for all absence of argument and inevitable endorsement of the step. If the whole of India responds or at least Delhi does, the fast might be soon ended.

No softness

But whether it ends soon or late or never, let there be no softness in dealing with what may be termed as a crisis. Critics have regarded some of my previous fasts as coercive and held that on merits the verdict would have gone against my stand but for the pressure exercised by the fasts. What value can an adverse verdict have when the purpose is demonstrably sound? A pure fast, like duty, is its own reward. I do not embark upon it for the sake of the result it may bring. I do so because I must. Hence, I urge everybody dispassionately to examine the purpose and let me die, if I must, in peace which I hope is ensured. Death for me would be a glorious deliverance, rather than that I should be a helpless witness of the destruction of India, Hinduism, Sikhism and Islam. That destruction is certain if Pakistan ensures no equality of status and security of life and property for all professing the various faiths of the world, and if India copies her. Only then Islam dies in the two Indias, not in the world. But Hinduism and Sikhism have no world outside India. Those who differ from me will be honoured by me for their resistance however implacable. Let my fast quicken conscience, not deaden it. Just contemplate the rot that has set in beloved India and you will rejoice to think that there is a humble son of hers who is strong enough and possibly pure enough to take the happy step. If he is neither, he is a burden on earth. The sooner he disappears and clears the Indian atmosphere of the burden, the better for him and all concerned.

I would beg of all friends not to rush to Birla House nor try to dissuade me or be anxious for me. I am in God's hands. Rather, they should turn the searchlights inwards, for this is essentially a testing time for all of us. Those who remain at their post of duty and perform it diligently and well, now more so than hitherto, will help me and the cause in every way. The fast is a process of self-purification.

Thoughts of Mahatma Gandhi

10

Non-violence and World Crisis

In my opinion, non-violence is not passivity in any shape or form. Non-violence, as I understand it, is the activist force in the world. Therefore, whether it is materialism or anything else, if non-violence does not provide an effective antidote, it is not the active force of my conception. Or, to put it conversely, if you bring me some conundrums that I cannot answer, I would say my non-violence is still defective. Non-violence is the supreme law. During my half a century of experience, I have not yet come across a situation when I had to say that I was helpless, that I had no remedy in terms of non-violence. Take the question of the Jews on which I have written. No Jew need feel helpless if he takes to the non-violent way. A friend has written me a letter, objecting, that in that article I have assumed that the Jews have been violent. It is true that the Jews have not been actively violent in their own persons. But they called down upon the Germans the curses of mankind, and they wanted America and England to fight Germany on their behalf. If I hit my adversary, that is of course violence, but to be truly non-violent, I must love him and pray for him, even when he hits me. The Jews have not been actively non-violent or, in spite of the misdeeds of the dictators, they would say: 'We shall suffer at their hand; they know no better, but we shall suffer not in the manner in which they want us to suffer.' If even one Jew acted thus, he would save his self-respect and leave an example which, if it became infectious, would save the whole of Jewry and leave a rich heritage to mankind besides. What about China, you will ask. The Chinese have no designs upon other people. They have no desire for territory. True, perhaps, China is not ready for such aggression; perhaps, what looks like her pacifism is only indolence. In any case, China's is not active non-violence. Her putting up a valiant defence against Japan is proof enough that China was never intentionally non-violent. That she is on the defensive is no answer in terms of non-violence. Therefore, when the time for testing her active non-violence came, she failed in the test. This is no criticism of China. I wish the Chinese success. According to the accepted standards, her behaviour is strictly correct. But when the position is examined in terms of non-violence, I must say it is unbecoming for a nation of 400 million, a nation as cultured as China, to repel Japanese aggression by resorting to Japan's own methods. If the Chinese had non-violence of my conception, there would be no use left for the latest machinery for destruction which Japan possesses. The Chinese would say to Japan: 'Bring all your machinery, we present half of our population to you. But the remaining 200 million won't bend their knee to you.' If the Chinese did that, Japan would become China's slave.

It has been objected, however, that non-violence is all right in the case of the Jews because there is personal contact between the individual and his persecutors, but in China, Japan comes with its long-range guns and aeroplanes. The person who rains death from above has never any chance of even knowing who and how many he has killed. How can non-violence combat aerial warfare, seeing that there are no personal contacts? The reply to this is that behind the death-dealing bomb, there is the human hand that releases it, and behind that still, is the human heart that sets the hand in motion. And at the back of the policy of terrorism is the assumption that terrorism, if applied in a sufficient measure, will produce the desired result, namely, bend the adversary to the tyrant's will. But supposing a people make up their mind that they will never do the tyrant's will, nor retaliate with the tyrant's own methods, the tyrant will not find it worth his while to go on with his terrorism. If sufficient food is given to the tyrant, a time will come when he will have had more than surfeit. If all the mice in the world held a conference together and resolved that they would no more fear the cat but all run into her mouth, the mice would live. I have actually seen a cat play with a mouse. She did not kill it outright but held it between her jaws, then released it, and again pounced upon it as soon as it made an effort to escape. In the end, the mouse died out of sheer fright. The cat would have derived no sport if the mouse had not tried to run away. I learnt the lesson of non-violence from my wife, when I tried to bend her to my will. Her determined resistance to my will on the one hand and her quiet submission to the suffering my stupidity involved on the other, ultimately made me ashamed of myself and cured me of my stupidity in thinking that I was born to rule over her, and in the end she became my teacher in non-violence. And what I did in South Africa was but an extension of the rule of satyagraha which she unwillingly practised in her own person.

Q. *You do not know Hitler and Mussolini. They are incapable of any kind of moral response. They have no conscience and they have made themselves impervious to world opinion. Would it not be playing into the hands of these dictators if, for instance, the Czechs, following your advice, confronted them with non-violence? Seeing that dictatorships are unmoral by definition, would the law of moral conversion hold good in their case?*

A. Your argument presupposes that the dictators like Mussolini or Hitler are beyond redemption. But belief in non-violence is based on the assumption that human nature in its essence is one and, therefore, unfailingly responds to the advances of love. It should be remembered that they have up to now always found ready response to the violence that they have used. Within their experience, they have not come across organized non-violent resistance on an appreciable scale, if at all. Therefore, it is not only highly likely, but I hold it to be inevitable, that they would recognize the superiority of non-violent resistance over any display of violence that they may be capable of putting forth. Moreover, the non-violent technique that I have presented to the Czechs does not depend for its success on the goodwill of the dictators; for, a non-violent resister depends upon the unfailing assistance of God which sustains him throughout difficulties which would otherwise be considered insurmountable. His faith makes him indomitable.

Suppose, they (dictators) come and occupy mines, factories and all sources of natural wealth belonging to the Czechs, then the following results can take place: (i) The Czechs may be annihilated for disobedience to orders. That would be a glorious victory for the Czechs and the beginning of the fall of Germany. (ii) The Czechs might become demoralized in the presence of overwhelming force. This is a result common in all struggles, but if demoralization does take place, it would not be on account of non-violence, but it would be due to absence or inadequacy of non-violence. (iii) The third thing that can take place is that Germany might use her new possessions for occupation by her surplus population. This, again, could not be avoided by offering violent resistance, for we have assumed that violent resistance is out of the question. Thus, non-violent resistance is the best method under all conceivable circumstances.

Q. *What can I, as a Christian, do to contribute to international peace? How can international anarchy be broken down and non-violence made effective for establishing peace? Subject nations apart, how can nations at the top be made to disarm themselves?*

A. You, as a Christian, can make an effective contribution by non-violent action even though it may cost you your all. Peace will never come until the Great Powers courageously decide to disarm themselves. It seems to me that recent events must force that belief on the Great Powers. I have an implicit faith—a faith that today burns brighter than ever, after half a century's experience of unbroken practice of non-violence—that mankind can only be saved through non-violence, which is the central teaching of the Bible as I have understood the Bible.

(Source: *Harijan*, 24 December 1938)

11

Non-violence vs Violence

In theory, if there is sufficient non-violence developed in any single person, he should be able to discover the means of combating violence, no matter how widespread or severe, within his jurisdiction. I have repeatedly admitted my imperfections. I am no example of perfect ahimsa. I am evolving. Such ahimsa as has been developed in me has been found enough to cope with situations that have hitherto arisen. But today, I feel helpless in the face of the surrounding violence. There was a penetrating article in *The Statesman* on my Rajkot statement. The editor therein contended that the English had never taken our movement to rue satyagraha, but being practical people, they had allowed the myth to continue though they had known it to be a violent revolt. It was none the less so because the rebels had no arms. I have quoted the substance from memory. When I read the article, I felt the force of the argument. Though I had intended the movement to be purely non-violent resistance, as I look back upon the happenings of those days, there was undoubtedly violence among the resisters. I must own that had I been perfectly tuned to the music of ahimsa, I would have sensed that the slightest departure from my sensitiveness would have rebelled against any discord in it.

It seems to me that the united action of the Hindus and

the Muslims led me to the violence that was lurking in the breasts of many. The English who are trained diplomats and administrators are accustomed to line of least resistance, and when they found that it was more profitable to conciliate a big organization than to crush it by extensive frightfulness, they yielded to the extent that they thought was necessary. It is, however, my conviction that our resistance was predominantly non-violent in action and will be accepted as such by the future historian. As a seeker of truth and non-violence, however, I must not be satisfied with mere action if it is not from the heart. I must declare from the housetops that the non-violence of those days fell far short of the violence as I have so often defined.

Non-violent action without the cooperation of the heart and the head cannot produce the intended result. The failure of our imperfect ahimsa is visible to the naked eye. Look at the feud that is going on between the Hindus and the Muslims. Each is arming for the fight with the other. The violence that we had harboured in our breasts during the non-cooperation is now recoiling upon ourselves. The violent energy that was generated among the masses, but was kept under check in the pursuit of common objective, has now been let loose and is being used among and against ourselves.

The same phenomenon is discernible, though in a less crude manner, in the dissension among Congressmen themselves and the use of forcible methods that the Congress ministers are obliged to adopt in running the administrations under their charge. This narrative clearly shows that the atmosphere is surcharged with violence. I hope it also shows that non-violent mass movement is an impossibility unless the atmosphere is radically changed. To blind one's eyes to the events happening around us is to court disaster. It has been suggested to me that I should declare mass civil disobedience and all internal strife will cease, the Hindus and the Muslims will compose their differences, Congressmen will forget mutual jealousies and fights for power. My reading of the situation is wholly different. If any mass movement is undertaken at the present moment in the name of non-violence, it will resolve itself into violence, largely unorganized, and organized in some cases. It will bring discredit on the Congress, spell disaster for the Congress struggle for Independence and bring ruin to many a home. This may be a wholly untrue picture born of my weakness. If so, unless I shed that weakness, I cannot lead a movement which requires great strength and resolution.

But if I cannot find an effective, purely non-violent method, outbreak of violence seems to be a certainty. The people demand self-expression. They are not satisfied with the constructive programme prescribed by me and accepted almost unanimously by the Congress. As I have said before, the imperfect response to the constructive programme is itself proof positive of the skin-deep nature of the non-violence of the Congressmen.

But, if there is an outbreak of violence, it would not be without cause. We are yet far from the independence of our dream. The irresponsibility of the Centre, which eats up 80 per cent of the revenue, grinds down the people and thwarts their aspirations, is daily proving more and more intolerable.

There is a growing consciousness of the terrible autocracy of the majority of the states. I admit my responsibility for the suspension of civil resistance in several states. This has resulted in demoralization both among the people and the princes. The people have lost nerve and feel that all is lost. The demoralization among the princes consists in their thinking that now they have nothing to fear from their people, nothing substantial to grant. Both are wrong. The result does not dismay me. In fact I had foretold the possibility of these results when I was discussing with Jaipur workers the advisability of suspending the movement, even though it was well circumscribed with rules and restrictions. The demoralization among the people shows that there was not non-violence in thought and word, and therefore, when the intoxication and excitement of jail-going and the accompanying demonstrations ceased, they thought that the struggle was over. The princes came to the hasty conclusion that they could safely consolidate their autocracy by adopting summary measures against the resisters and placating the docile element by granting eyewash reforms.

Both the people and the princes might have reacted in the right manner—the people by recognizing the correctness of my advice and calmly generating strength and energy by quiet and determined constructive effort, and the princes by seizing the opportunity, afforded by suspension, of doing justice for the sake of justice and granting reforms that would satisfy the reasonable but advanced section among their people. This could only happen if they recognized the time spirit. It is neither too late for the people nor the princes.

In this connection I may not omit the Paramount Power. There are signs of the Paramount Power repenting of the recent declarations about the freedom to the princes to grant such reforms to their people as they chose. There are audible whispers that the princes may not take those declarations literally. It is an open secret that the princes dare not do anything that they guess is likely to displease the

Paramount Power. They may not even meet persons whom the Paramount Power may not like them to meet. When there is this tremendous influence exercised over the princes, it is but natural to hold the Paramount Power responsible for the unadulterated autocracy that reigns supreme in many states.

So, if violence breaks out in this unfortunate land, the responsibility will have to be shared by the Paramount Power, the princes, and above all by the Congressmen. The first two have never claimed to be non-violent. Their power is frankly derived from and based on the use of violence. But the Congress has since 1920 adopted non-violence as its settled policy and has undoubtedly striven to act up to it. But as the Congressmen never had non-violence in their hearts, they must reap the fruit of the defect, however unintentional it was. At the crucial moment, the defect has come to the surface and the defective method does not seem to meet the situation. Non-violence is never a method of coercion, it is one of conversion. We have failed to convert the princes, we have failed to convert the English administrators. It is no use saying that it is impossible to persuade persons willingly to part with their power. I have claimed that satyagraha is a new experiment. It will be time to pronounce it a failure when the Congressmen have given it a genuine trial. Even a policy, if it is honestly pursued, has to be pursued with all one's heart. We have not done so. Hence, the Congressmen have to convert themselves before the Paramount Power and the princes can be expected to act justly.

But if the Congressmen can or will go no further than they have done in the direction of non-violence, and if the Paramount Power and the princes do not voluntarily and selfishly do the right thing, the country must be prepared for violence, unless the new technique yields a new mode of non-violent action which will become an effective substitute for violence as a way of securing redress of wrongs. The fact that violence must fail will not prevent its outbreak. Mere constitutional agitation will not do.

(Source: *Harijan*, 4 July 1938)

12

Religion vs No Religion

A correspondent writes:

'In the *Harijanbandhu* of the 5th May, you have written that your non-violence contemplates destruction of animals dangerous to mankind, such as leopards, wolves, snakes, scorpions, etc.

'You do not believe in giving food to dogs, etc. Several other people besides the Gujaratis look upon the feeding of dogs as a meritorious act. Such a belief may not be justifiable in times of food shortage like the present. Yet we must remember that these animals can be very useful to man. One can feed them and take work out of them.

'You had put twenty-seven questions to Shri Raichandbhai from Durban. One of these questions was: "What should a seeker do when a snake attacks him?" His answer was: "He should not kill the snake and, if it bites, he should let to do so." How is it that you speak differently now?'

I have written a lot on this subject in the past. At that time, the topic was the killing of rabid dogs. There was much discussion on the subject, but all that seems to have been forgotten.

My non-violence is not merely kindness to all living creatures. The emphasis laid on the sacredness of subhuman life in Jainism is understandable. But that can never mean that one is to be kind to this life in preference to human life. While writing about the sacredness of such life, I take it that the sacredness of human life has been taken for granted. The former has been overemphasized. And, while putting it into practice, the idea has undergone distortion. For instance, there are many who derive complete satisfaction in feeding ants. It would appear that the theory has become a wooden, lifeless dogma. Hypocrisy and distortion are passing current in the name of religion.

Ahimsa is the highest ideal. It is meant for the brave, never for the cowardly. To benefit by others' killing and delude oneself into the belief that one is being very religious and non-violent is sheer self-deception.

A so-called votary of non-violence will not stay in a village which is visited by a leopard every day. He will run away and, when someone has killed the leopard, will return to take charge of his hearth and home. This is not non-violence. This is a coward's violence. The man who has killed the leopard has at least given proof of some bravery. The man who takes advantage of the killing is a coward. He can never expect to know true non-violence.

In life, it is impossible to eschew violence completely. The question arises, where is one to draw the line? The line cannot be the same for everyone. Although essentially the principle is the same, yet, everyone applies it in his or her own way. What is one man's food can be another's poison. Meat-eating is a sin for me. Yet, for another person, who has always lived on meat and never seen anything wrong in it, to give it up simply in order to copy me will be a sin.

If I wish to be an agriculturist and stay in the jungle, I will have to use the minimum unavoidable violence in order to protect my fields. I will have to kill monkeys, birds and insects that eat up my crops. If I do not wish to do so myself, I will have to engage someone to do it for me. There is not much difference between the two. To allow crops to be eaten up by animals in the name of ahimsa while there is a famine in the land is certainly a sin. Evil and good are relative terms. What is good under certain conditions can become an evil or a sin under a different set of conditions.

Man is not to drown himself in the well of shastras, but he is to dive in their broad ocean and bring out pearls. At every step, he has to use his discrimination as to what is ahimsa and what is himsa (violence). In this, there is no room for shame or cowardice. The poet has said that the road leading up to God is for the brave, never for the cowardly. Finally, Raichandbhai's advice to me was that if I had courage, if I wanted to see God face to face, I should let myself be bitten by a snake, instead of killing it. I have never killed a snake before or after receiving that letter. That is no matter of credit for me. My ideal is to be able to play with snakes and scorpions fearlessly. But it is merely a wish so far. Whether and when it will be realized I do not know. Everywhere I have let my people kill both. I could have prevented them if I had wished. But how could I? I did not have the courage to take them up with my own hands and teach my companions a lesson in fearlessness. I am ashamed that I could not do so. But my shame could not benefit them or me.

If Ramanama favours me, I might still attain that courage someday. In the meantime, I consider it my duty to act as I have stated above. Religion is a thing to be lived. It is not mere sophistry.

(Source: *Harijan*, 29 May 1946)

13

The Doctrine of the Sword

In this age of the rule of brute force, it is almost impossible for anyone to believe that anyone else could possibly reject the law of final supremacy of brute force. And so I receive anonymous letters advising me that I must not interfere with the progress of non-cooperation, even though popular violence may break out. Others come to me and assuming that secretly I must be plotting violence, inquire when the happy moment for declaring open violence will arrive. They assure me that the English never yield to anything but violence—secret or open. Yet others I am informed, believe that I am the most rascally person living in India because I never give out my real intention and that they have not a shadow of a doubt that I believe in violence just as much as most people do.

Such being the hold that the doctrine of the sword has on the majority of mankind, and as success of non-cooperation depends principally on absence of violence during its pendency and as my views in this matter affect the conduct of a large number of people. I am anxious to state them as clearly as possible.

I do believe that where there is only a choice between cowardice and violence, I would advise violence. Thus when my eldest son asked me what he should have done, had he been present when I was almost fatally assaulted in 1908, whether he should have run away and seen me killed or whether he should have used his physical force which he could and wanted to use, and defended me, I told him that it was his duty to defend me, even by using violence. Hence, it was that I took part in the Boer War, the so-called Zulu Rebellion and the late War. Hence also do I advocate training in arms for those who believe in the method of violence. I would rather have India resort to arms in order to defend her honor than that she should in a cowardly manner become or remain a helpless witness to her own dishonour.

But I believe that non-violence is infinitely superior to violence; forgiveness is more manly than punishment, forgiveness adorns a soldier. But abstinence is forgiveness only when there is the power to punish; it is meaningless when it pretends to proceed from a helpless creature. A mouse hardly forgives a cat when it allows itself to be torn to pieces by her. I, therefore, appreciate the sentiment of those who cry out for the condign punishment of General Dyer and his ilk. They would tear him to pieces if they could. But I do not believe myself to be a helpless creature. Only I want to use India's and my strength for better purpose.

Let me not be misunderstood. Strength does not come from physical capacity. It comes from an indomitable will. An average Zulu is any way more than a match for an average Englishman in boldly capacity. But he flees from an English boy, because he fears the boy's revolver or those who will use it for him. He fears death and is nerveless in spite of his burly figure. We in India may in moment realize that one hundred thousand Englishmen need not frighten three hundred million human beings. A definite forgiveness would, therefore, mean a definite recognition of our strength. With enlightened forgiveness must come a mighty wave of strength in us, which would make it impossible for a Dyer and a Frank Johnson to heap affront upon India's devoted head. It matters little to me that for the moment I do not drive my point home. We feel too downtrodden not to be all angry and revengeful. But I must not refrain from a saying that India can gain more by waiving the right of punishment. We have better work to do, a better mission to deliver to the world.

I am not a visionary. I claim to be a practical idealist. The religion of non-violence is not meant merely for the rishis and saints. It is meant for the common people as well. Non-violence is the law of our species as violence is the law of the brute. The spirit lies dormant in the brute and he knows no law but that of physical might. The dignity of man requires obedience to a higher law to the strength of the spirit.

I have, therefore, ventured to place before India the ancient law of self-sacrifice. For satyagraha and its off-shoots, non-cooperation and civil resistance are nothing but new names for the law of suffering. The rishis, who discovered the law of non-violence in the midst of non-violence, were greater geniuses than Newton. They were themselves greater warriors than Wellington. Having themselves known the use of arms, they realized their uselessness and taught a weary world that its salvation may not be through non-violence.

Non-violence in its dynamic condition means conscious suffering. It does not mean meek submission to the will of the evil-doer, but it means the putting of one's whole soul against the will of the tyrant. Working under this law of being, it is possible for a single individual to defy the whole might of an unjust empire to save his honor, his religion, his soul and lay the foundation for the empire's fall or its regeneration.

And so I am not pleading for India to practise non-violence because it is weak. I want her to practise non-violence being conscious of her strength and power. No training in arms is required for the realization of her strength. We seem to need it because we seem to think that we are but a lump of flesh. I want India to recognize that she has a soul that cannot perish and that can rise triumphant above every physical weakness and defy the physical combination of a whole world. What is the meaning of Rama, a mere human being, with his host of monkeys, pitting himself against the insolent strength of the ten-headed Ravan surrounded in supposed safety by the raging waters on all sides of Lanka? Does it not mean the conquest of physical might by spiritual strength? However being a practical man, I do not wait till India recognizes the practicability of the spiritual life in the political world. India considers herself to be powerless and paralyzed before the machine guns, the tanks and the aeroplanes of the English. And she takes up non-cooperation out of her weakness. It must still be the same purpose namely, bring her delivery from the crushing weight of British injustice if a sufficient number of people practice it.

I isolate this non-cooperation from Sinn Féinism, for, it is so conceived as to be incapable of being offered side by side with violence. But I invite even the school of violence to give this peaceful non-cooperation a trial. It will not fail through its inherent weakness. It may fail because of poverty of response. Then will be one time for real danger. The high-souled men, who are unable to suffer national humiliation any longer, will want to vent their wrath. They will take to violence. So far as I know, they must perish without delivering themselves or their country from the wrong. If India takes up the doctrine of the sword, she may gain momentary victory. Then India will cease to be the pride of my heart. I am wedded to India because I owe my all to her. I believe absolutely that she has a mission for the world. She is not to copy Europe blindly. India's acceptance of the doctrine of the sword will be the hour of my trial. I hope I shall not be found wanting. My religion has no geographical limits. If I have a living faith in it, it will transcend my love for India herself. My life is dedicated to the service of India through the religion of non-violence which I believed to be the root of Hinduism. Meanwhile I urge those who distrust me, not to disturb the even working of the struggle that has just commenced, by inciting to violence in the belief that I want violence. I detest secrecy as a sin. Let them give non-violent non-cooperation a trial and they will find that I had no mental reservation whatsoever.

(Source: *Young India*, Ahmedabad,
Wednesday, 11 August 1920)

14

Resistance to Aggression

I must live. I would not be a vassal to any nation or body. I must have absolute independence or perish. To seek to win in a clash of arms would be pure bravado. Not so if, in defying the might of one who would deprive me of my independence, I refuse to obey his will and perish unarmed in the attempt. In so doing, though I lose the body, I save my soul, i.e., my honour.

Duty of resistance

The true democrat is he who with purely non-violent means defends his liberty, and therefore, his country's, and ultimately, that of the whole of mankind... But the duty of resistance accrues only to those who believe in non-violence as a creed—not to those who will calculate and will examine the merits of each case and decide whether to approve of or oppose a particular war. It follows that such resistance is a matter for each person to decide for himself and under the guidance of the inner voice, if he recognizes its existence.

◆

The use of non-violence

The true meaning of non-resistance has often been misunderstood or even distorted. It never implies that a non-violent man should bend before the violence of an aggressor. While not returning the latter's violence by violence, he should refuse to submit to the latter's illegitimate demand even to the point of death. That is the true meaning of non-resistance... He is not to return violence by violence, but neutralize it by withholding one's hand and, at the same time, refusing to submit to the demand. This is the only civilized way of going on in the world. Any other course can only lead to a race for armaments interspersed by periods of peace which is by necessity and brought about by exhaustion, when preparations would be going on for violence of a superior order. Peace through superior violence inevitably leads to the atom bomb and all that it stands for. It is the complete negation of non-violence and of democracy which is not possible without the former.

To answer brutality with brutality is to admit one's moral and intellectual bankruptcy and it can only start a vicious circle...

◆

Resistance, both forms—passive resistance and non-violent resistance—are, but you have to pay a very heavy price when your resistance is passive, in the sense of the weakness of the resister. Europe mistook the bold and brave resistance, full of wisdom, by Jesus of Nazareth, for passive resistance, as if it was of the weak. As I read the New Testament for the first time, I detected no passivity, no weakness about Jesus as depicted in the four gospels, and the meaning became clearer to me when I read Tolstoy's *Harmony of the Gospels* and his other kindred writings. Has not the West paid heavily in regarding Jesus as a Passive Resister? Christendom has been responsible for the wars which put to shame even those described in the Old Testament and other records, historical or semi-historical. I know that I speak under correction, for I can but claim very superficial knowledge of history—modern or ancient.

◆

To die without killing requires more heroism (than to die in the act of killing). There is nothing very wonderful in killing and being killed in the process. But the man who offers his neck to the enemy for execution, but refuses to bend to his will, shows courage of a far higher type.

15

The Way of Ahimsa

Ahimsa is one of the world's greatest principles which no power on earth can wipe out. Thousands, like myself, may die in trying to vindicate the ideal, but ahimsa will never die. And the gospel of ahimsa can be spread only through believers dying for the cause.

Ahimsa is the highest ideal. It is meant for the brave, never for the cowardly. To benefit by others' killing, and delude oneself into the belief that one is being very religious and non-violent is sheer self-deception.

◆

No power on earth can subjugate you when you are armed with the sword of ahimsa. It ennobles both the victor and the vanquished.

◆

The proper way to view the present outburst of violence throughout the world is to recognize that the technique of unconquerable non-violence of the strong has not been at all fully discovered as yet. Not an ounce of non-violent strength is ever wasted.

◆

I do not say 'eschew violence in you dealing with robbers or thieves or with nations that may invade India.' But, in order that we are better able to do so, we must learn to restrain ourselves. It is a sign not of strength but of weakness to take up the pistol on the slightest pretext. Mutual fisticuffs are a training not in violence but in emasculation.

◆

Whilst all violence is bad and must be condemned in the abstract, it is permissible for—it is even the duty of—a believer in ahimsa to distinguish between the aggressor and the defender. Having done so, he will side with the defender in a non-violent manner, i.e., give his life in saving him. His intervention is likely to bring a speedier end to the duel, and may even result in bringing about peace between the combatants.

◆

My non-violence does recognize different species of violence—defensive and offensive. It is true that in the long run, the difference is obliterated, but the initial merit persists. A non-violent person is bound, when the occasion arises, to say which side is just. Thus, I wished success to the Abyssinians, the Spaniards, the Czechs, the Chinese and the Poles, though in each case I wished that they could have offered non-violent resistance.

If war is itself a wrong act, how can it be worthy of moral support or blessings? I believe all war to be wholly wrong. But, if we scrutinize the motives of two warring parties, we may find one to be in the right and the other in the wrong. For instance, if A wishes to seize B's country, B is obviously the wronged one. Both fight with arms. I do not believe in violent warfare, but all the same, B, whose cause is just, deserves my moral help and blessings.

You can return blow for blow if you are not brave enough to follow the path of non-violence. But there is a moral code for the use of violence also. Otherwise, the very flames of violence will consume those who light them. I do not care if they are all destroyed. But I cannot countenance the destruction of India's freedom.

I have recognized that the nation has the right, if it so wills, to vindicate her freedom, even by actual violence. Only, then India ceases to be the land of my love, even though the land of my birth, even as I should take no pride in my mother if she went astray.

When India becomes self-supporting, self-reliant and proof against temptations and exploitation, she will cease to be the object of greedy attraction for any power in the West or the East and will then feel secure without having to carry the burden of expensive armaments. Her internal economy will be the strongest bulwark against aggression.

16

Non-violent Resistance

History has no record of a nation having adopted non-violent resistance. If Hitler is unaffected by my suffering, it does not matter. For I shall have lost nothing of worth. My honour is the only thing worth preserving. That is independent of Hitler's pity. But as a believer in non-violence, I may not limit its possibilities. Hitherto he and his likes have built upon their invariable experience that men yield to force. Unarmed men, women and children offering non-violent resistance without any bitterness in them will be a novel experience for them. Who can dare say that it is not in their nature to respond to the higher and finer forces? They have the same soul that I have... I have a call I must answer. I must deliver my message to my people. This humiliation has sunk too deep in me to remain without an outlet. I, at least, must act up to the light that has dawned on me... When I first launched out on satyagraha, I had no companion. We were 13,000 men, women and children against a whole nation, capable of crushing the existence out of us. I did not know who would listen to me. It all came as in a flash. All the 13,000 did not fight. Many fell back. But the honour or the nation was saved. New history was written by the South African satyagraha... My purpose will be fulfilled if I succeed in reaching these men's hearts and making them see that, if their non-violence does not make them feel much braver than the possession of arms and the ability to use them, they must give up their non-violence, which is another name for cowardice, and resume their arms which there is nothing but their own will to prevent them from taking back. I present a weapon not of the weak but of the brave. There is no bravery greater than a resolute refusal to bend the knee to an earthly power, no matter how great, and that without bitterness of spirit and in the fullness of faith that the spirit alone lives, nothing else does.

17

Never Doubt Non-violence

I have argued from the analogy of what we do in families or even clans. The humankind is one big family. And if the love expressed is intense enough, it must apply to all mankind. If individuals have succeeded even with savages, why should not a group of individuals succeed with a group, say, of savages? If we can succeed with the English, surely it is merely an extension of faith to believe that we are likely to succeed with less cultured or less liberally minded nations. I hold that, if we succeed with the English with unadulterated non-violent effort, we must succeed with the others, which is the same thing as saying, that, if we achieve freedom with non-violence, we shall defend it also with the same weapon. If we have not achieved that faith, our non-violence is a mere expedient; it is the alloy, not pure gold. In the first place, we shall never achieve freedom with doubtful non-violence; and in the second, even if we do, we shall find ourselves wholly unprepared to defend the country against an aggressor. If we have doubt about the final efficacy of non-violence, it would be far better for the Congress to revise its policy and invite the nation to training in arms. A mass organization like the Congress will be untrue to its charge if, not knowing its own mind, it misled the people into a false belief. It would be an act of cowardice... Because we cease to pin our faith to non-violence, we do not necessarily become violent. We merely throw off the mask and be natural. It would be a perfectly dignified course to adopt.

◆

However small a nation or even a group may be, it is able, even as the individual, provided that it has one mind as also the will and the grit, to defend its honour and self-respect against a whole world in arms. Therein consists the matchless strength and beauty of the unarmed. That is non-violent defence which neither knows nor accepts defeat at any stage. Therefore, a nation or a group which has made non-violence its final policy cannot be subjected to slavery, even by the atom bomb.

◆

The Congress has declared that she would carry out the struggle for India's independence through the method of non-violence. But she has not yet decided whether she would adhere to that method for the protection of that freedom against possible foreign aggression. To me, it is a self-evident truth that, if freedom is to be shared equally by all—even physically the weakest, the lame and the halt—they must be able to contribute an equal share in its defence. How that can be possible when reliance is placed on armaments my plebian mind fails to understand. I, therefore, swear and shall continue to swear by non-violence, i.e., by satyagraha or soul force. In it, physical incapacity is no handicap and even a frail woman or a child can pit herself or himself on equal terms against a giant, armed with the most powerful weapon.

◆

My ahimsa forbids me from denying credit where it is due, even though the creditor is a believer in violence. Thus, though I did not accept Subhash Bose's belief in violence and his consequent action, I have not refrained from giving unstinted praise to his patriotism, resourcefulness and bravery. Similarly, though I did not approve of the use of arms by the union government for aiding the Kashmiris, and though I could not approve of Sheikh Abdullah's resort to arms, I cannot possibly withhold admiration for either for their resourceful and praiseworthy conduct, especially if both the relieving troops and the Kashmiri defenders die heroically to a man. I know that if they can do so, they will perhaps change the face of India. But if the defence is purely non-violent in intention and action, I will not use the word 'perhaps', for I will be sure of change in the face of India, even to the extent of converting to the defender's view the union Cabinet, if not even the Pakistan Cabinet.

The non-violent technique, I will suggest, will be no armed assistance to the defenders. Non-violent assistance can be sent from the union without stint. But the defenders, whether they get such assistance or not, will defy the might of the raiders or even a disciplined army in overwhelming numbers. And defenders dying at their post of duty without malice and without anger in their hearts against the assailants, and without the use of any arms, including even their fists will mean an exhibition of heroism as yet unknown to history. Kashmir will then become a holy land shedding its fragrance not only throughout India, but the world.

18

The Choice before India

I am not pleading for India to practice non-violence because it is weak. I want her to practice non-violence being conscious of her strength and power. No training in arms is required for realization of her strength. We seem to need it because we seem to think that we are a lump of flesh.

◆

India has to make her choice. She may try, if she wishes, the way of war and sink lower than she has... If India can possibly gain her freedom by war, her state will be no better and will be, probably, much worse than that of France or England...

◆

The way of peace

But the way of peace is open to her. Her freedom is assured if she has patience. That way will be found to be the shortest, even though it may appear to be the longest to our impatient nature. The way of peace insures internal growth and stability. We reject it because we fancy that it involves submission to the will of the ruler who has imposed himself upon us. But the moment we realize that the imposition is only so called and that, through our unwillingness to suffer loss of life or property, we are party to the imposition, all we need do is to change that negative attitude of passive endorsement. The suffering to be undergone by the change will be nothing compared to the physical suffering and the moral loss we must insure in trying the way of war. And the sufferings of war harm both the parties. The sufferings in following the way of peace must benefit both. They will be like the pleasurable travail of a new birth... The way of peace is the way of truth. Truthfulness is even more important than peacefulness. Indeed, lying is the mother of violence. A truthful man cannot long remain violent. He will perceive in the course of his search that he has no need to be violent, and he will further discover that, so long as there is the slightest trace of violence in him, he will fail to find the truth he is searching.

◆

Non-violence is not an easy thing to understand, still less to practice, weak as we are. We must all act prayerfully and humbly and continually asking God to open the eyes of our understanding, being ever ready to act according to the light as we daily receive it. My task as a lover and promoter of peace, therefore, today consists in unflinching devotion to non-violence in the prosecution of the campaign for regaining our liberty. And if India succeeds in so regaining our liberty and if India succeeds in so regaining it, it will be the greatest contribution to world peace.

19

No Imitation of the West

The fashion nowadays is to take for granted that whatever America and England are doing is good enough for us... War has become a matter of money and resourcefulness in inventing weapons of destruction. It is no longer a matter of personal bravery or endurance. To compass the destruction of men, women and children, it might be enough for me to press a button and drop poison on them in a second.

Do we wish to copy this method of defending ourselves? Even if we do, have we the financial ability? We complain of ever-growing military expenditure. But if we would copy America or England, we would have to increase the burden tenfold...

The nation cannot be kept on the non-violent path by violence. It must grow from within to the state it may aspire to. The question, therefore, for us to consider is: What is our immediate aspiration? Do we first want to copy the Western nations, and then, in the demand distant future, after having gone through the agony, retrace our steps? Or, do we want to strike out an original path, or rather retain what to me is our own predominantly peaceful path and there through win and assert our freedom?

Here there is no question of compromise with cowardice. Either we train and arm ourselves for destruction, be it in self-defence, and in the process train for suffering too, or we merely prepare ourselves for suffering for defending the country or delivering it from domination. In either case, bravery is indispensable. In the first case, personally, bravery is not of such importance as in the second. In the second case, too, we shall perhaps never be able to do without violence altogether. But violence then will be subservient to non-violence and will always be a diminishing factor in national life. At the present moment, though the national sentiment is non-violence, in thought and word at least, we seem to be drifting towards violence. Impatience pervades the atmosphere. We are restrained from violence through our weakness. What is wanted is a deliberate giving up of violence out of strength. To be able to do this requires imagination coupled with a penetrating study of the world drift. Today, the superficial glamour of the West dazzles us, and we mistake for progress the giddy dance which engages us from day to day. We refuse to see that it is surely leading us to death. Above all, we must recognize that to compete with the Western nations on their terms is to court suicide. Whereas, if we realize that, notwithstanding the seeming supremacy of violence, it is the moral force that governs the universe, we should train for non-violence with the fullest faith in its limitless possibilities. Everybody recognizes that, if a non-violent atmosphere had been maintained in 1922, we could have completely gained our end. Even as it is, we had a striking demonstration of the efficacy of non-violence, crude though it was, and the substance of swaraj then gained has never been lost. The paralyzing fear that had possessed the nation before the advent of satyagraha has gone once for all. In my opinion, therefore, non-violence is a matter of patient training. If we are to be saved and are to make a substantial contribution to the world's progress, ours must emphatically and predominantly be the way of peace.

20

Alternative to War

I feel in the innermost recesses of my heart, after a political experience extending over an unbroken period of close upon thirty-five years, that the world is sick unto death of blood-spilling. The world is seeking a way out, and I flatter myself with the belief that, perhaps, it will be the privilege of the ancient land of India to show that way out to the hungering world. I have, therefore, no hesitation whatsoever in inviting all the great nations of the earth to give their hearty co-operation to India in her mighty struggle.

21

India and the Creed of Non-violence

I venture to suggest, in all humility, that if India reaches her destiny through truth and non-violence, she will have made no small contribution to world peace for which all the nations of the earth are thirsting and she would also have, in that case, made some slight return for the help that those nations have been freely giving to her.

If in the glow of freedom, India could live up to that creed of non-violence, non-dependence on physical force, no power on earth would ever cast an evil eye upon her. This would be India's crowning glory and her contribution to the world's progress.

22

Non-violence of the Brave

Our non-violence has brought us to the gate of Independence. Shall we renounce it after we have entered that gate? I, for one, am firmly convinced that non-violence of the brave, such as I have envisaged, provides the surest ad most efficacious means to face foreign aggression and internal disorder just as it has done for winning independence. A truly non-violent India will have nothing to fear from any foreign power, nor will it look to British navy and air force for her defence. I know that we have not as yet the non-violence of the brave.

23

The Significance of Non-violence for India

I see clearly that, if the country cannot be turned to non-violence, it will be bad for it and the world. It will mean goodbye to freedom. It might even mean a military dictatorship. I am day and night thinking how non-violence of the brave can be cultivated. I said at the Asiatic Conference that I hoped the fragrance of the non-violence of India would permeate the whole world. I often wonder if that hope will materialize.

24

India's Duty

India is now free, and the reality is now clearly revealed to me. Now that the burden of subjection has been lifted, all the forces of good have to be marshaled in one great effort to build a country which forsook the accustomed method of violence in order to settle human conflicts, whether it is between two states or between two sections of the same people. I have yet the faith that India will rise to the occasion and prove to the world that the birth of two new states will be not a menace, but a blessing to the rest of mankind. It is the duty of Free India to perfect the instrument of non-violence for dissolving collective conflicts, if its freedom is going to be really worthwhile.

◆

[Non-violence] has enabled a mighty nation of forty crores to shake off the foreign yoke without bloodshed. It is the freedom of India that has brought freedom to Burma and Ceylon. A nation that has won freedom without the force of arms should be able to keep it, too, without the force of arms. This in spite of the fact that India has an army, a navy in the making and an air force, and these are being developed still further. I am convinced that, unless India develops her non-violent strength, she has gained nothing either for herself or for the world. Militarization of India will mean her own destruction as well as the whole world.

25

The Way to Peace

Disarmament

I do suggest that the doctrine [of non-violence] holds good also as between states and states. I know that I am treading on delicate ground if I refer to the late War. But I fear I must, in order to make the position clear. It was a war of aggrandizement, as I have understood, on either part. It was a war for dividing the spoils of the exploitation of weaker races—otherwise euphemistically called the world commence... It would be found that, before general disarmament in Europe commences, as it must someday unless Europe is to commit suicide, some nation will have to dare to disarm herself and take large risks. The level of non-violence in that nation, if that event happily comes to pass, will naturally have risen so high as to command universal respect. Her judgements will be unerring, her decision firm, her capacity for heroic self-sacrifice will be great, and she will want to live as much for other nations as for herself.

◆

Like opium production, the world manufacture of swords needs to be restricted. The sword is probably responsible for more misery in the world than opium.

26

What Should a Neutral State Do?

'Since disarmament chiefly depends on Great Power, why should Switzerland, which is a small state and a neutral state, be asked to disarm itself?'

It is from the neutral ground of your country that I am speaking to all other powers and not only to Switzerland. If you won't carry this message to other parts of Europe, I shall be absolved from all blame. And seeing that Switzerland is a neutral territory and non-aggressive nation, there is all the more reason why Switzerland should not need an army. Secondly, it is through your hospitality and by reason of your occupying the vantage ground that you have nationals coming to you. It should be possible for you to give to the world a lesson on disarmament and show that you are brave enough to do without an army.

◆

How could a disarmed neutral country allow other nations to be destroyed? But for our army which was waiting ready at our frontier during the last war we should have been ruined.

At the risk of being considered a visionary or a fool, I must answer this question in the only manner I know. It would be cowardly of a neutral country to allow an army to devastate a neighbouring country. But there are two ways in common between soldiers of war and soldiers of non-violence, and if I had been a citizen of Switzerland and president of the federal state, what I would have done would be to refuse passage to the invading army by refusing all supplies. Secondly, by reenacting a Thermopylx in Switzerland, you would have presented a living wall of men and woman and children, inviting invaders to walk over your corpses. You may say that such a thing is beyond human experience and endurance. I say that it is not so. It was quite possible. Last year in Gujarat, women stood lathi-charges unflinchingly, and in Peshawar, thousands stood hails of bullets without resorting to violence. Imagine these men and women staying in front of an army requiring a safe passage to another country. The army would be brutal enough to walk over them, you might say. I would then say you will still have done your duty by allowing yourself to be annihilated. An army that dares to pass over the corpses of innocent men and women would not be able to repeat that experiment. You may, if you wish, refuse to believe in such courage on the part of the masses of men and women, but then, you would have to admit that non-violence is made of sterner stuff. It was never conceived as a weapon of the weak but of the stoutest hearts.

27

Great Power and Disarmament

It is... open to the Great Powers to take it [non-violence] up any day and cover themselves with glory and earn the eternal gratitude of posterity. If they or any of them could shed the fear of destruction, if they disarmed themselves, they will automatically help the rest to regain their sanity. But then, these Great Powers have to give up imperialistic ambitions and the exploitation of the so-called uncivilized or semi-civilized nations of the earth and revise their mode of life. It means a complete revolution. Great nations can hardly be expected, in the ordinary course, to move spontaneously in a direction the reverse of the one they have followed, and according to their notion of values, from victory to victory. But miracles have happened before and may happen even in this very prosaic age. Who can dare limit God's power of undoing wrong? One thing is certain. If the mad race for armaments continues, it is bound to result in a slaughter such as has never occurred in history. If there is a victor left, the very victory will be a living death for the nation that emerges victorious. There is no escape from the impending doom save through a bold and unconditional acceptance of the non-violent method with all its glorious implications.

28

Gangsterism vs Non-violence

'What to do with "gangster" nations, if I may the expression frequently used? There was individual gangsterism in America. It has been put down by strong police measures, both local and national. Could not we do something similar for gangsterism between nations, as instanced in Manchuria—the nefarious use of the opium poison, in Abyssinia, in Spain, in the sudden seizure of Austria, and then, the case of Czechoslovakia?' If the best minds of the world have not imbibed the spirit of non-violence, they would have to meet gansterism in the orthodox way. But that would only show that we have not got far beyond the law of the jungle, that we have not yet learnt to appreciate the heritage that God has given us, that, in spite of the teaching of Christianity which is 1,900 years old and of Hinduism and Buddhism which are older, and even of Islam (if I have read it aright), we have not made much headway as human beings. But, whilst I would understand the use of force by those who have not the spirit of non-violence to throw their whole weight in demonstrating that even gangsterism has to be met by non-violence. For, ultimately, force, however justifiably used, will lead us into the same morass as the force of Hitler and Mussolini. There will be just a difference of degree. You and I who believe in non-violence must use it at the critical moment. We may not despair of touching the hearts even of gangsters, even if, for the moment, we may seem to be striking our heads against a blind wall.

29

Non-violent Alternative

When the position is examined in terms of non-violence, I must say it is unbecoming of a great nation of 400 million, a nation as cultured as China, to repel Japanese aggression by resorting to Japan's own methods. If the Chinese had non-violence of my conception, there would be no use left for the latest machinery for destruction which Japan possesses. The Chinese would say to Japan, 'Bring all your machinery, we present half of our population to you. But, the remaining 200 million won't bend their knee to you'. If the Chinese did that, Japan would become China's slave.

◆

...For the Poles to stand valiantly against the German hordes, vastly superior in numbers, military equipment and strength, was almost non-violence. I should not mind repeating that statement over and over again. You must give its full value to the word 'almost'. But we are 400 million here. If we were to organize a big army and prepare ourselves to fight foreign aggression, how could we by any stretch of imagination call ourselves *almost* non-violent, let alone non-violent? The Poles were unprepared for the way in which the enemy swooped down upon them. When we talk of armed preparation, we contemplate preparation to meet any violent combination with our superior violence. If India ever prepared herself that way, she would constitute the greatest menace to world peace. For, if we take that path, we will also have to choose the path of exploitation like the European nations.

30

Peace through Love

It may be long before the law of love will be recognized in international affairs. The machineries of governments stand between and hide the hearts of one people from those of another. Yet...we can see how the world is moving steadily to realize that between nation and nation, as between man and man, force has failed to solve problems, but that the economic sanction of non-cooperation is far more mighty and conclusive than armies and navies.

◆

Till a new energy is harnessed and put on wheels, the captains of older energies will treat the innovation as theoretical, impractical, idealistic, and so on. It may take long to lay the wires for international love, but the sanction of international non-cooperation in preference to continued physical compulsion...is a distinct progress towards the ultimate and real solution.

31

Enduring Peace

Not to believe in the possibility of permanent peace is to disbelieve in the Godliness of human nature. Methods hereto adopted have failed because rock-bottom sincerity on the part of those who have striven has been lacking. Not that they have realized this lack. Peace is unattained by part performance of conditions, even as a chemical combination is impossible without complete fulfillment of the conditions of attainment thereof. If the recognized leaders of mankind who have control over the engines of destruction were wholly to renounce their use, with full knowledge of its implications, permanent peace can be obtained. This is clearly impossible without the Great Powers of the earth renouncing their imperialistic design. This, again, seems impossible without great nations ceasing to believe in soul-destroying competition and to desire to multiply wants and, therefore, increase their material possessions. It is my conviction that the root of the evil is want of a living faith in a living God. It is a first-class human tragedy that peoples of the earth who claim to believe in the message of Jesus, whom they describe as the Prince of Peace, show little of that belief in actual practice. It is painful to see sincere Christian divines limiting the scope of Jesus' message to select individuals. I have been taught from my childhood and tested the truth by experience that the primary virtues of mankind are possible of cultivation by the meanest of the human species. It is this undoubted universal possibility that distinguishes the humans from the rest of God's creation. If even one nation were unconditionally to perform the supreme act of renunciation, many of us would see in our lifetime visible peace established on earth.

(Message to *Cosmopolitan*, New York)

◆

Peace will never come until the Great Powers courageously decide to disarm themselves. It seems to me that recent events must force that belief on the Great Powers. I have an implicit faith, a faith that today burns brighter than ever, after half-a-century's experience of unbroken practice of non-violence, that mankind can only be saved through non-violence which is the central teaching of the Bible as I have understood the Bible.

32

No 'Appeasement'

I have never admitted any partiality for 'appeasement' which has become a term of reproach in the English language. Peace I want among all mankind, but I do not want peace at any cost, and certainly not by placating the aggressor or at the cost of honour. Anyone, therefore, who thinks that I am guilty of either vice will do great harm to the immediate purpose.

◆

My experience, daily growing stronger and richer, tells me that there is no peace for individuals or for nations without practicing truth and non-violence to the uttermost extent possible for man. The policy of retaliation has never succeeded.

33

Non-violent Society

It has become the fashion these days to say that society cannot be organized or run on non-violent lines. I join issue on that point. In a family, when a father slaps his delinquent child, the latter does not think of retaliating. He obeys his father not because of the deterrent effect of the slap, but because of the offended love which he senses behind it. That, in my opinion, is an epitome of the way in which society is or should be governed. What is true of the family must be true of society which is but a larger family.

34

End to War

I reiterate my conviction that there will be no peace for the allies or the world unless they shed their belief in the efficacy of war and its accompanying terrible deception and fraud and are determined to hammer out real peace based on freedom and equality of all races and nations. Exploitation and domination of one nation over another can have no place in a world striving to put an end to all wars. In such a world only, the militarily weaker nations will be free from the fear of intimidation or exploitation.

◆

Not to return violence by violence but neutralize it by withholding one's hand and, at the same time, refusing to submit to the [aggressor's] demand [backed by force] is the only civilized way of going on in the world. Any other course can only lead to a race for armaments, interspersed by periods of peace which is by necessity and brought about by exhaustion, when preparations will be going on for violence of a superior order. Peace through superior violence inevitably leads to the atom bomb and all that it stands for. It is the complete negation of non-violence and of democracy which is not possible without the former.

◆

I can say with confidence that if the world is to have peace, non-violence is the means to that end and no other.

35

Pacifism and Pacifists

A true pacifist is a true satyagrahi. The latter acts by faith and, therefore, is not concerned about the result, for he knows that it is assured when the action is true... Pacifists have to prove their faith by resolutely refusing to do anything with war, whether of defence or offence.

◆

Pacifists have to live their lives in strict accord with the Sermon on the Mount, and they will find immediately that there is much to give up and much to remodel. The greatest thing that they have to deny themselves is the fruit of imperialism...

36

The Gospel of Non-violence

The law of our species

I am not a visionary. I claim to be a practical idealist. The religion of non-violence is not meant merely for the rishis and saints. It is meant for the common people as well. Non-violence is the law of our species as violence is the law of the brute. The spirit lies dormant in the brute and he knows no law but that of physical might. The dignity of man requires obedience to a higher law to the strength of the spirit... The rishis who discovered the law of non-violence in the midst of violence were greater geniuses than Newton. They were themselves known to the use of arms, they realized their uselessness and taught a weary world that its salvation lay not through violence but through non-violence.

◆

My ahimsa

I know only one way—the way of ahimsa. The way of himsa goes against my grain. I do not want to cultivate the power to inculcate himsa... The faith sustains me that He is the help of the helpless, that He comes to one's succor only when one throws himself on His mercy. It is because of that faith that I cherish the hope that God will one day show me a path which I may confidently commend to the people.

◆

I have been a 'gambler' all my life. In my passion for finding truth and in relentlessly following out my faith in non-violence, I have counted no stake too great. In doing so, I have erred, if at all, in the company of the most distinguished scientist of any age and any clime.

◆

The doctrine that has guided my life is not one of inaction but of the highest action.

◆

I must not, therefore, flatter myself with the belief—nor allow friends like you to entertain the belief that I have exhibited any heroic and demonstrable non-violence in myself. All I can claim is that I am sailing in that direction without a moment's stop.

37

Character of Non-violence

Non-violence is the law of the human race and is infinitely greater than and superior to brute force. In the last resort, it does not avail to those who do not possess a living faith in the God of Love. Non-violence affords the fullest protection to one's self-respect and sense of honour, but not always to possession of land or movable property, though its habitual practice does prove a better bulwark than the possession of armed men to defend them. Non-violence, in the very nature of things, is of no assistance in the defence of ill-gotten gains and immoral acts. Individuals or nations who would practice non-violence must be prepared to sacrifice (nations to last man) their all, except honour. It is, therefore, inconsistent with the possession of other people's countries, i.e., modern imperialism, which is frankly based on force for its defence. Non-violence is a power which can be wielded equally by all—children, young men and women or grown-up people—provided they have a living faith in the God of Love and have, therefore, equal love for all mankind. When non-violence is accepted as the law of life, it must pervade the whole being and not be applied to isolated acts. It is a profound error to suppose that, whilst the law is good enough for individuals, it is not for the masses of mankind.

◆

For, the way of non-violence and truth is sharp as the razor's edge. Its practise is more than our daily food. Rightly taken, food sustains the body; rightly practised non-violence sustains the soul. The body food we can only take in measured quantities and at stated intervals; non-violence, which is the spiritual food, we have to take in continually. There is no such thing as satiation. I have to be conscious every moment that I am pursuing the goal and have to examine myself in terms of that goal.

38

Changeless Creed

The very first step in non-violence is that we cultivate in our daily life, as between ourselves, truthfulness, humility, tolerance, loving kindness. Honesty, they say in English, is the best policy. But, in terms of non-violence, it is not a mere policy. Policies may and do change. Non-violence is an unchangeable creed. It has to be pursued in face of violence raging around you. Non-violence with a non-violent man is no merit. In fact, it becomes difficult to say whether it is non-violence at all. But when it is pitted against violence, then one realizes the difference between the two. This we cannot do unless we are ever wakeful, ever vigilant, ever striving.

◆

The only thing lawful is non-violence. Violence can never be lawful in the sense meant here, i.e., not according to man-made law but according to the law made by nature for man.

39

Faith in God

[A living faith in non-violence] is impossible without a living faith in God. A non-violent man can do nothing save by the power and grace of God. Without it, he won't have the courage to die without anger, without fear and without retaliation. Such courage comes from the belief that God sits in the hearts of all and that there should be no fear in the presence of God. The knowledge of the omnipresence of God also means respect for the lives, even of those who may be called opponents...

◆

Non-violence is an active force of the highest order. It is the soul force or the power of God-head within us. An imperfect man cannot grasp the whole of that Essence; he would not be able to bear its full blaze, but even an infinitesimal fraction of it, when it becomes active within us, can work wonders. The sun in the heavens fills the whole universe with its life-giving warmth. But if one went too near it, it would consume him to ashes. Even so it is with God-head. We become Godlike to the extent we realize non-violence; but we can never become wholly God.

◆

The fact is that non-violence does not work in the same way as violence. It works in the opposite way. An armed man naturally relies upon his arms. A man who is intentionally unarmed relies upon the Unseen Force called God by poets, but called the Unknown by scientists. But that which is unknown is not necessarily non-existent. God is the Force among all forces known and unknown. Non-violence without reliance upon that Force is poor stuff to be thrown in the dust.

◆

Consciousness of the living presence of God within one is undoubtedly the first requisite.

40

Religious Basis

My claim to Hinduism has been rejected by some, because I believe and advocate non-violence in its extreme form. They say that I am a Christian in disguise. I have been even seriously told that I am distorting the meaning of the Gita, when I ascribe to that great poem the teaching of unadulterated non-violence. Some of my Hindu friends tell me that killing is a duty enjoined by the Gita under certain circumstances. A very learned shastri only the other day scornfully rejected my interpretation of the Gita and said that there was no warrant for the opinion held by some commentators that the Gita represented the eternal duel between the forces of evil and good, and inculcated the duty of eradicating evil within us without hesitation, without tenderness. I state these opinions against non-violence in detail, because it is necessary to understand them, if we would understand the solution I have to offer... I must be dismissed out of considerations. My religion is a matter solely between my Maker and myself. If I am a Hindu, I cannot cease to be one, even though I may be disowned by the whole of the Hindu population. I do, however, suggest that non-violence is the end of all religions.

◆

The lesson of non-violence is present in every religion, but I fondly believe that, perhaps, it is here in India that its practice has been reduced to a science. Innumerable saints have laid down their lives in tapashcharya until poets had felt that the Himalayas became purified in their snowy whiteness by means of their sacrifice. But all this practice of non-violence is nearly dead today. It is necessary to revive the eternal law of answering anger by love and of violence by non-violence; and where can this be more readily done than in this land of Kind Janaka and Ramachandra?

41

Hinduism's Unique Contribution

Non-violence is common to all religions, but it has found the highest expression and application in Hinduism. (I do not regard Jainism or Buddhism as separate from Hinduism). Hinduism believes in the oneness not of merely all human life but in the oneness of all that lives. Its worship of the cow is, in my opinion, its unique contribution to the evolution of humanitarianism. It is a practical application of the belief in the oneness and, therefore, sacredness of all life. The great belief in transmigration is a direct consequence of that belief. Finally, the discovery of the law of Varnashrama is a magnificent result of the ceaseless search for truth.

◆

I have also been asked wherefrom in Hinduism I have unearthed ahimsa. Ahimsa is in Hinduism, it is in Christianity as well as in Islam. Whether you agree with me or not, it is my bounden duty to preach what I believe to be the truth as I see it. I am also sure that ahimsa has never made anyone a coward.

42

The Koran and Non-violence

[Barisaheb] assured me that there was warrant enough for satyagraha in the Holy Koran. He agreed with the interpretation of the Koran to the effect that, whilst violence under certain well-defined circumstances is permissible, self-restraint is dearer to God than violence, and that is the law of love. That is satyagraha. Violence is concession to human weakness, satyagraha is an obligation. Even from the practical standpoint, it is easy enough to see that violence can do no good and only do infinite harm.

◆

Some Muslim friends tell me that Muslims will never subscribe to unadulterated non-violence. With them, they say, violence is as lawful and necessary as non-violence. The use of either depends upon circumstances. It does not need Koranic authority to justify the lawfulness of both. That is the well-known path the world has traversed through the ages. There is no such thing as unadulterated violence in the world. But I have heard it from many Muslim friends that the Koran teaches the use of non-violence. It regards forbearance as superior to vengeance. The very word 'Islam' means 'peace', which is non-violence. Badshah Khan, a staunch Muslim who never misses his namaz and Ramzan, has accepted out-and-out non-violence as his creed. It would be no answer to say that he does not live up to his creed, even as I know to my shame that I do not. If there is difference in our actions, the difference is not one of kind, it is of degree. But, the argument about non-violence in the Holy Koran is an interpolation, not necessary for my thesis.

43

No Matter of Diet

Ahimsa is not a mere matter of dietetics; it transcends it. What a man eats or drinks matters little; it is the self-denial, the self-restraint behind it that matters. By all means, practise as much restraint in the choice of the articles of your diet as you like. The restraint is commendable, even necessary, but it touches only the fringe of ahimsa. A man may allow himself a wide latitude in the matter of diet and yet may be a personification of ahimsa and compel our homage, if his heart overflows with love and melts at another's woe, and has been purged of all passions. On the other hand, a man always over-scrupulous in diet is an utter stranger to ahimsa and pitiful wretch, if he is a slave to selfishness and passions and is hard of heart.

44

Road to Truth

My love for non-violence is superior to every other thing mundane or supramundane. It is equaled only by my love for truth, which is to me synonymous with non-violence through which and which alone I can see and reach truth.

◆

Without ahimsa it is not possible to seek and find truth. Ahimsa and truth are so intertwined that it is practically impossible to disentangle and separate them. They are like the two sides of a coin, or rather of a smooth, unstamped, metallic disc. Who can say which the obverse is, and which is the reverse? Nevertheless ahimsa is the means; truth is the end. Means to be means must always be within our reach, and so ahimsa is our supreme duty. If we take care of the means, we are bound to reach the end sooner of latter. When once we have grasped this point, final victory is beyond question.

◆

Ahimsa is not the goal. Truth is the goal. But we have no means of realizing truth in human relationships except through the practice of ahimsa. A steadfast pursuit of ahimsa is inevitably bound to truth—not so violence. That is why I swear by ahimsa. Truth came naturally to me. Ahimsa I acquired after a struggle. But ahimsa being the means, we are naturally more concerned with it in our everyday life. It is ahimsa, therefore, that our masses have to be educated in. Education in truth follows from it as a natural end.

45

No Cover for Cowardice

My non-violence does not admit of running away from danger and leaving dear ones unprotected. Between violence and cowardly flight, I can only prefer violence to cowardice. I can no more preach non-violence to a coward than I can tempt a blind man to enjoy healthy scenes. Non-violence is the summit of bravery. And in my own experience, I have had no difficulty in demonstrating to men trained in the school of violence the superiority of non-violence. As a coward, which I was for years, I harboured violence. I began to prize non-violence only when I began to shed cowardice. Those Hindus who ran away from the post of duty when it was attended with danger did so not because they were non-violent, or because they were afraid to strike, but because they were unwilling to die or even suffer an injury. A rabbit that runs away from the bull terrier is not particularly non-violent. The poor thing trembles at the sight of the terrier and runs for very life.

◆

Non-violence is not a cover for cowardice, but it is the supreme virtue of the brave. Exercise of non-violence requires far greater bravery than that of swordsmanship. Cowardice is wholly inconsistent with non-violence. Translation from swordsmanship to non-violence is possible and, at times, even an easy stage. Non-violence, therefore, presupposes the ability to strike. It is a conscious deliberate restraint put upon one's desire for vengeance. But vengeance is any day superior to passive, effeminate and helpless submission. Forgiveness is higher still. Vengeance, too, is weakness. The desire for vengeance comes out of fear of harm, imaginary or real. A dog barks and bites when he fears. A man who fears no one on earth would consider it too troublesome even to summon up anger against one who is vainly trying to injure him. The sun does not wreak vengeance upon little children who throw dust at him. They only harm themselves in the act.

◆

The path of true non-violence requires much more courage than violence.

◆

The minimum that is required of a person wishing to cultivate the ahimsa of the brave is first to clear one's thought of cowardice and, in the light of the clearance, regulate his conduct in every activity, great or small. Thus the votary must refuse to be cowed down by his superior, without being angry. He must, however, be ready to sacrifice his post, however remunerative it may be. Whilst sacrificing his all, if the votary has no sense of irritation against his employer, he has ahimsa of the brave in him. Assume that a fellow-passenger threatens my son with assault and I reason with the would-be-assailant who then turns upon me. If then I take his blow with grace and dignity, without harbouring any ill will against him, I exhibit the ahimsa of the brave. Such instances are of everyday occurrence and can be easily multiplied. If I succeed in curbing my temper every time and, though able to give blow for blow, I refrain, I shall develop the ahimsa of the brave which will never fail me and which will compel recognition from the most confirmed adversaries.

◆

Inculcation of cowardice is against my nature. Ever since my return from South Africa, where a few thousand had stood up not unsuccessfully against heavy odds, I have made it my mission to preach true bravery which ahimsa means.

46

Humility Essential

If one has pride and egoism, there is no non-violence. Non-violence is impossible without humility. My own experience is that, whenever I have acted non-violently, I have been led to it and sustained in it by the higher promptings of an unseen power. Through my own will I should have miserably failed. When I first went to jail, I quailed at the prospect. I had heard terrible things about jail life. But I had faith in God's protection. Our experience was that those who went to jail in a prayerful spirit came out victorious, those who had gone in their own strength failed. There is no room for self-pitying in it either when you say God is giving you the strength. Self-pity comes when you do a thing for which you expect recognition from others. But there is no question of recognition.

◆

It was only when I had learnt to reduce myself to zero that I was able to evolve the power of satyagraha in South Africa.

The power of non-violence

Non-violence in its dynamic condition means conscious suffering. It does not mean meek submission to the will of the evil-doer, but it means the pitting of one's whole soul against the will of the tyrant. Working under this law of our being, it is possible for a single individual to defy the whole might of an unjust empire to save his honour, his religion, his soul and lay the foundation for that empire's fall or its regeneration.

47

Active Force

The non-violence of my conception is a more active and more real fighting against wickedness than retaliation whose very nature is to increase wickedness. I contemplate a mental and, therefore, a moral opposition to immoralities. I seek entirely to blunt the edge of the tyrant's sword, not by putting up against it a sharper-edged weapon, but by disappointing his expectation that I would be offering physical resistance. The resistance that I should offer instead would elude him. It would at first dazzle him, and at last compel recognition from him, which recognition would not humiliate him but would uplift him. It may be urged that this again is an ideal state. And so it is. The propositions from which I have drawn my arguments are as true as Euclid's definitions, which are none the less true because in practice, we are unable to even draw Euclid's line on a blackboard. But even a geometrician finds it impossible to get on without bearing in mind Euclid's definitions. Nor may we dispense with the fundamental propositions on which the doctrine of satyagraha is based.

I admit that the strong will rob the weak and that it is a sin to be weak. But this is said of the soul in man, not of the body. If it be said of the body, we could never be free from the sin of weakness. But the strength of the soul can defy a whole world in arms against it. This strength is open to the weakest in body.

Non-violence is the greatest force at the disposal of mankind. It is mightier than the mightiest weapon of destruction devised by the ingenuity of man. Destruction is not the law of the humans. Man lives freely by his readiness to die, if need be, at the hands of his brother, never by killing him. Every murder or other injury, no matter for what cause, committed or inflicted on another is a crime against humanity.

Non-violence is like radium in its action. An infinitesimal quantity of it embedded in a malignant growth acts continuously, silently and ceaselessly till it has transformed the whole mass of the diseased tissue into a healthy one. Similarly, even a little of true non-violence acts in a silent, subtle, unseen way and leavens the whole society.

48

Matchless Bravery

An armed soldier relies on his weapons for his strength. Take away from him his weapons—his gun or his sword, and he generally becomes helpless. But a person who has truly realized the principle of non-violence has the God-given strength for his weapon and the world has not known anything that can match it.

A small body of determined spirits fired by an unquenchable faith in their mission can alter the course of history.

Non-violence of the strong is any day stronger than that of the bravest soldier fully armed or a whole host.

49

Exercise in Faith

The hardest metal yields to sufficient heat. Even so the hardest heart must melt before sufficiency of the heat of non-violence. And there is no limit to the capacity of non-violence to generate heat.

Every action is a resultant of a multitude of forces even of a contrary nature. There is no waste of energy. So we learn in the books on mechanics. This is equally true of human actions. The difference is that in the one case we generally know the forces at work, and when we do, we can mathematically foretell the resultant. In the case of human actions, they result from a concurrence of forces of most of which we have no knowledge. But our ignorance must not be made to serve the cause of disbelief in the power of these forces. Rather is our ignorance a cause for greater faith. And non-violence being the mightiest force in the world and also the most elusive in its working, it demands the greatest exercise of faith. Even as we believe in God in faith, so have we to believe in non-violence in faith.

Violence, like water when it has an outlet, rushes forward furiously with an overwhelming force. Non-violence cannot act madly. It is the essence of discipline. But, when it is set going, no amount of violence can crush it. For full play, it requires unsullied purity and an unquenchable faith...

50

A Science

Ahimsa is a science. The word 'failure' has no place in the vocabulary of science. Failure to obtain the expected result is often the precursor to further discoveries.

◆

If the function of himsa is to devour all it comes across, the function of ahimsa is to rush into the mouth of himsa. In an atmosphere of ahimsa, one has no scope to put his ahimsa to the test. It can be tested only in the face of himsa.

◆

Violence can only be effectively met by non-violence. This is an old, established truth...that the weapon of violence, even if it was the atom bomb, became useless when matched against non-violence. That very few understand how to wield this mighty weapon is true. It requires a lot of understanding and strength of mind. It is unlike what is needed in military schools and colleges. The difficulty one experiences in meeting himsa with ahimsa arises from weakness of the mind.

51

The Deed, not Doer

'Hate the sin and not the sinner' is a precept which, though easy enough to understand, is rarely practised, and that is why the poison of hatred spreads in the world. This ahimsa is the basis of the search for truth. I am realizing every day that the search is vain unless it is founded on ahimsa as the basis. It is quite proper to resist and attack a system, but to resist and attack its author is tantamount to resisting and attacking oneself. For we are all tarred with the same brush, and are children of one and the same creator, and as such, the divine powers within us are infinite. To slight a single human being is to slight those divine powers, and thus to harm not only that Being but with Him the whole world.

Man and his deed are two distinct things. Whereas a good deed should call forth approbation and a wicked deed disapprobation, the doer of the deed, whether good or wicked, always deserves respect or pity as the case may be.

Those who seek to destroy men rather than manners adopt the latter and become worse than those whom they destroy under the mistaken belief that the manners will die with the men. They do not know the root of the evil.

◆

It is the acid test of non-violence that, in a non-violent conflict, there is no rancor left behind, and in the end, the enemies are converted into friends. That was my experience in South Africa, with General Smuts. He started with being my bitterest opponent and critic. Today he is my warmest friend.

◆

The principal implication of ahimsa is that the ahimsa in us ought to soften and not to stiffen our opponents' attitude to us; it ought to melt him; it ought to strike a responsive chord in his heart.

As ahimsa-ites, can you say that you practise genuine ahimsa? Can you say that you receive the arrows of the opponent on your bare breasts without returning them? Can you say that you are not angry, that you are not perturbed by his criticism?

◆

By reason of lifelong practise of ahimsa, I claim to be an expert in it, though very imperfect. Speaking in absolute terms, the more I practise it, the clearer I see how far I am from the full expression of ahimsa in my life. It is his ignorance of this, the greatest duty of man in the world, which makes him say that in this age non-violence has little scope in the face of violence, whereas I make bold to say that in this age of the atom bomb, unadulterated non-violence is the only force that can confound all the tricks put together of violence.

52

Training for Non-violence

How are we to train individuals or communities in this difficult art?

There is no royal road, except through living the creed in your life which must be a living sermon. Of course, the expression in one's own life presupposes great study, tremendous perseverance, and thorough cleansing of one's self of all the impurities. If for mastering of the physical sciences you have to devote a whole lifetime, how many lifetimes may be needed for mastering the greatest spiritual force that mankind has known? But why worry, even if it means several lifetimes? For, if this is the only permanent thing in life, if this is the only thing that counts, then whatever effort you bestow on mastering it is well spent. Seek ye first the Kingdom of Heaven and everything else shall be added unto you. The Kingdom of Heaven is ahimsa.

Arms are surely unnecessary for a training in ahimsa. In fact, the arms, if any, have to be thrown away, as the Khansaheb did in the Frontier Province. Those who hold that it is essential to learn violence before we can learn non-violence would hold that only sinners can be saints.

53

Fearlessness: the Prerequisite

Just as one must learn the art of killing in the training for violence, so one must learn the art of dying in the training for non-violence. Violence does not mean emancipation from fear, but discovering the means of combating the cause of fear. Non-violence, on the other hand, has no cause for fear. The votary of non-violence has to cultivate the capacity for sacrifice of the highest type in order to be free from fear. He racks not if he should lose his land, his wealth, his life. He who has not overcome all fear cannot practise ahimsa to perfection. The votary of ahimsa has only one fear—that is of God. He who seeks refuge in God ought to have a glimpse of the atman that transcends the body; and the moment one has a glimpse of the imperishable atman, one sheds the love of the perishable body. Training in non-violence is thus diametrically opposed to training in violence. Violence is needed for the protection of things external, non-violence is needed for the protection of the atman, for the protection of one's honour. This non-violence cannot be learnt by staying at home. It needs enterprise. In order to test ourselves, we should learn to dare danger and death, mortify the flesh and acquire the capacity to endure all manner of hardships. He who trembles or take to his heels the moment he sees two people fighting is not non-violent, but a coward. A non-violent person will lay down his life in preventing such quarrels. The bravery of the non-violent is vastly superior to that of the violent. The badge of the violent is his weapon-spear, or sword, or rifle. God is the shield of the non-violent. This is not the course of training for one intending to learn non-violence. But it is easy to evolve one from the principles I have laid down.

54

Non-violence of the Brave

Non-violence does not require any outside or outward training. It simply requires the will not to kill even in retaliation and the courage to face death without revenge. This is no sermon on ahimsa but cold reason and the statement of a universal law. Given the unquenchable faith in the law, no provocation should prove too great for the exercise of forbearance. This I havc described as the non-violence of the brave.

That non-violence which only an individual can use is not of much use in terms of society. Man is a social being. His accomplishments to be of use must be such as any person with sufficient diligence can attain. That which can be exercised only among friends is of value only as a spark of non-violence. It cannot merit the appellation of ahimsa. 'Enmity vanishes before ahimsa' is a great aphorism. It means that the greatest enmity requires an equal measure of ahimsa for its abatement. Cultivation of this virtue may need long practise, ever extending to several births. It does not become useless on that account. Traveling along the route, the pilgrim will meet richer experiences from day to day, so that he may have a glimpse of the beauty he is destined to see at the top. This will add to his zest. No one is entitled to infer from this that the path will be a continuous carpet of roses without thorns.

A poet has sung that the way to reach God accrues only to the very brave, never to the faint-hearted. The atmosphere today is so much saturated with poison that one refuses to recollect the wisdom of the ancients and to perceive the varied little experience of ahimsa in action. 'A bad turn is neutralized by a good' is a wise saying of daily experience in practice. Why can we not see that if the sum total of the world's activities was destructive, it would have come to an end long ago? Love, otherwise ahimsa, sustains this planet of ours. This much must be admitted. The precious grace of life has to be strenuously cultivated, naturally so because it is uplifting. Descent is easy not so ascent. A large majority of us being undisciplined, our daily experience is that of fighting or swearing at one another on the slightest pretext. This, the richest grace of ahimsa, will descend easily upon the owner of hard discipline.

55

Application of Non-violence

If one does not practise non-violence in one's personal relations with others, and hopes to use it in bigger affairs, one is vastly mistaken. Non-violence—like charity—must begin at home.

But if it is necessary for the individual to be trained in non-violence, it is even more necessary for the nation to be trained likewise. One cannot be non-violent in one's own circle and violent outside it. Or else, one is not truly non-violent even in one's own circle; often the non-violence is only in appearance. It is only when you meet with resistance, as for instance, when a thief or a murderer appears, that your non-violence is put on its trail. You either try or should try to oppose the thief with his own weapons, or you try to disarm him by love. Living among decent people, your conduct may not be described as non-violent. Mutual forbearance is non-violence. Immediately, therefore, you get the conviction that non-violence is the law of life, you have to practise it towards those who act violently towards you, and the law must apply to nations as individuals. Training no doubt is necessary. And beginnings are always small. But if the conviction is there, the rest will follow.

56

Universality of Non-violence

Non-violence to be a creed has to be all-pervasive. I cannot be non-violent about one activity of mine and violent about others.

It is a blasphemy to say that non-violence can only be practised by individuals and never by nations which are composed of individuals.

In my opinion, non-violence is not passivity in any shape or form. Non-violence, as I understand it, is the most active force in the world... Non-violence is the supreme law. During my half a century of experience, I have not yet come across a situation when I had to say that I was helpless, that I had no remedy in terms of non-violence.

57

Cultivation of Non-violence

I am an irrepressible optimist. My optimism rests on my belief in the infinite possibilities of the individual to develop non-violence. The more you develop it in your own being, the more infectious it becomes till it overwhelms your surroundings and by and by might oversweep the world.

I have known from early youth that non-violence is not a cloistered virtue to be practised by the individual for his peace and final salvation, but it is a rule of conduct for society if it is to live consistently with human dignity and make progress towards the attainment of peace for which it has been yearning for ages past.

To practise non-violence in mundane matters is to know its true value. It is to bring heaven upon earth. There is no such thing as the other world. All works are one. There is no 'here' and no 'there.' As Jeans has demonstrated, the whole universe including the most distant stars, invisible even through the most powerful telescope in the world, is compressed in an atom. I hold it, therefore, to be wrong to limit the use of non-violence to cave-dwellers and for acquiring merit for a favoured position in the other world. All virtue ceases to have use if it serves no purpose in every walk of life.

58

Use on Mass Scale

Unfortunately for us, we are strangers to the non-violence of the brave on a mass scale. Some even doubt the possibility of the exercise of non-violence by groups, much less by masses of people. They restrict its exercise to exceptional individuals. Only, mankind can have no use of it if it is always reserved only for individuals.

59

Efficacy

I have been practising with scientific precision non-violence and its possibilities for an unbroken period of over fifty years. I have applied it in every walk of life—domestic, institutional, economic and political. I know of no single case in which it has failed. Where it has seemed sometimes to have failed, I have ascribed it to my imperfections. I claim no perfection for myself. But I do claim to be a passionate seeker after truth, which is but another name for God. In the course of that search, the discovery of non-violence came to me. Its spread is my life's mission. I have no interest in living except for the prosecution of that mission.

There is no hope for the aching world except through the narrow and straight path of non-violence. Millions like me may fail to prove the truth in their own lives; that would be their failure, never of the eternal law.

60

The Non-violent Society

I hold that non-violence is not merely a personal virtue. It is also a social virtue to be cultivated, like the other virtues. Surely society is largely regulated by the expression of non-violence in its mutual dealings. What I ask for is an extension of it on a larger, national and international scale.

All society is held together by non-violence, even as the earth is held in her position by gravitation. But when the law of gravitation was discovered, the discovery yielded results of which our ancestors had no knowledge. Even so, when society is deliberately constructed in accordance with the law of non-violence, its structure will be different in material particulars from what it is today. But I cannot say in advance what the government based on non-violence will be like.

What is happening today is disregard of the law of non-violence and enthronement of violence as if it were an eternal law.

Society based on non-violence can only consist of groups settled in villages in which voluntary co-operation is the condition of dignified and peaceful existence.

61

The Government

The government cannot succeed in becoming entirely non-violent, because it represents all the people. I do not today conceive of such a golden age. But I do believe in the possibility of a predominantly non-violent society. And I am working for it.

There remains the question as to whether in an ideal society there should be any or no government. I do not think we need worry ourselves about this at the moment. If we continue to work for such a society, it will slowly come into being to an extent, such that the people can benefit by it. Euclid's line is one without breadth, but no one has so far been able to draw it and never will. All the same, it is only by keeping the ideal line in mind that we have made progress in Geometry. What is true here is true of every ideal.

62

Anarchy

It must be remembered that nowhere in the world does a state without government exist. If at all it could ever come into being, it would be in India; for, ours is the only country where the attempt has, at any rate, been made. We have not yet been able to show that bravery to the degree which is necessary and for the attainment of which there is only one way. Those who have faith in the latter have to demonstrate it. In order to do so, the fear of death has to be completely shed, just as we have shed the fear of prisons.

63

Democracy and Non-violence

Science of war leads one to dictatorship—pure and simple. Science of non-violence can alone lead one to pure democracy.

Democracy and violence can ill go together. The states that are today nominally democratic have either to become frankly totalitarian, or if they are to become truly democratic, they must become courageously non-violent.

Holding the view that, without the recognition of non-violence on a national scale, there is no such thing as a constitutional or democratic government, I devote my energy to the propagation of non-violence as the law of our life—individual, social, political, national and international. I fancy that I have seen the light, though dimly. I write cautiously for I do not profess to know the whole of the law. If I know the success of my experiments, I know also my failures. But the successes are enough to fill me with undying hope.

I have often said that if one takes care of the means, the end will take care of itself. Non-violence is the means; the end for everyone is complete independence. There will be an international league only when all the nations, big or small, composing it are fully independent. The nature of that independence will correspond to the extent of non-violence assimilated by the nations concerned. One thing is certain. In a society based on non-violence, the smallest nation will feel as tall as the tallest. The idea of superiority and inferiority will be wholly obliterated...

The conclusion is irresistible that for one like me, wedded to non-violence, constitutional or democratic government is a distant dream so long as non-violence is not recognized as a living force, an inviolable creed, not a mere policy. While I prate about universal non-violence, my experiment is confined to India. If it succeeds, the world will accept it without effort. There is however a bit BUT. The pause does not worry me. My faith is brightest in the midst of impenetrable darkness.

64

Use of Power

By its very nature, non-violence cannot 'seize' power, nor can that be its goal. But non-violence can do more; it can effectively control and guide power without capturing the machinery of government. That is its beauty. There is an exception, of course. If the non-violent non-cooperation of the people is so complete that the administration ceases to function or if the administration crumbles under the impact of a foreign invasion and a vacuum results, the people's representatives will then step in and fill it.

Theoretically that is possible. But the use of power need not necessarily be violent. A father wields power over his children; he may even punish but not by inflicting violence. The most effective exercise of power is that which irks least. Power rightly exercised must sit light as a flower; no one should feel the weight of it. The people accepted the authority of the Congress willingly. I was on more than one occasion invested with the absolute power of dictatorship. But everybody knew that my power rested on their willing acceptance. They could set me aside at any time and I would have stepped aside without a murmur. Prophets and supermen are born only once in an age. But if even a single individual realizes the ideal of ahimsa in its fullness, he covers and redeems the whole society. Once Jesus had blazed the trail, his twelve disciples could carry on his mission without his presence. It needed the perseverance and genius of so many generations of scientists to discover the laws of electricity, but today everybody, even children, use electric power in their daily life. Similarly, it will not always need a perfect being to administer an ideal state once it has come into being. What is needed is a thorough social awakening to begin with. The rest will follow. To take an instance nearer home, I have presented to the working class the truth that true capital is not silver or gold, but the labour of their hands and feet and their intelligence. Once labor develops that awareness, it would not need my presence to enable it to make use of the power that it will release.

65

The Non-violent State

Many have shaken their heads as they have said, 'But you can't teach non-violence to the masses. It is only possible for individuals and that too in rare cases.' That is, in my opinion, a gross self-deception. If mankind was not habitually non-violent, it would have been self-destroyed ages ago. But in the duel between forces of violence and non-violence, the latter have always come out victorious in the end. The truth is that we have not had patience enough to wait and apply ourselves whole-heartedly to the spread of non-violence among the people as a means for political ends.

66

Political Power

To me, political power is not an end but one of the means of enabling people to better their condition in every department of life. Political power means capacity to regulate national life through national representatives. If national life becomes so perfect as to become self-regulated, no representation becomes necessary. There is then a state of enlightened anarchy. In such a state, everyone is his own ruler. He rules himself in such a manner that he is never a hindrance to his neighbour. In the ideal state, therefore, there is no political power because there is no state. But the ideal is never fully realized in life. Hence the classical statement of Thoreau that the government is best which governs the least.

67

Capitalism: a Trusteeship

It is my firm conviction that if the state suppressed capitalism by violence, it will be caught in the coils of violence itself, and fail to develop non-violence at any time. The state represents violence in a concentrated and organized form. The individual has a soul, but as the state is a soulless machine, it can never be weaned from violence to which it owes its very existence. Hence I prefer the doctrine of trusteeship. The fear is always there that the state may use too much violence against those who differ from it. I would be very happy, indeed, if the people concerned behaved as trustees; but if they fail, I believe we shall have to deprive them of their possessions through the state with the minimum exercise of violence. That is why I said at the Round Table Conference that every vested interest must be subjected to scrutiny, and confiscation ordered where necessary with or without compensation as the case demanded. What I would personally prefer would be not centralization of power in the hands of the state, but an extension of the sense of trusteeship, as, in my opinion, the violence of private ownership is less injurious than the violence of the state. However, if it is unavoidable, I would support a minimum of state-ownership. While admitting that man actually lives by habit, I hold that it is better for him to live by the exercise of will. I also believe that men are capable of developing their will to an extent that will reduce exploitation to a minimum. I look upon an increase in the power of the state with the greatest fear because, although while apparently doing good by minimizing exploitation, it does the greatest harm to mankind by destroying individuality, which lies at the root of the progress. We know of so many cases where men have adopted trusteeship, but not where the state has really lived for the poor.

68

Non-violent Swaraj

In swaraj based on ahimsa, people need not know their rights, but it is necessary for them to know their duties. There is no duty but creates a corresponding right, and those only are true rights which flow from a due performance of one's duties. Hence, rights of true citizenship accrue only to those who serve the state to which they belong. And they alone can do justice to the rights that accrue to them. Everyone possesses the right to tell lies or resort to goondaism. But the exercise of such right is harmful both to the exerciser and society. But to him who observes truth and non-violence comes prestige, and prestige brings rights. And people who obtain rights as a result of performance of duty, exercise them only for the service of society, never for themselves. Swaraj of a people means the sum total of the swaraj of individuals. And such swaraj comes only from performance by individuals of their duty as citizens. In it, no one thinks of his rights. They come, when they are needed, for better performance of duty.

Under swaraj based on non-violence, nobody is anybody's enemy, everybody contributes his or her due quota to the common goal, all can read and write, and their knowledge keeps growing from day to day. Sickness and disease are reduced to the minimum. No one is a pauper and labour can always find employment. There is no place under such a government for gambling, drinking and immorality or for class hatred. The rich will use their riches wisely and usefully, and not squander them in increasing their pomp and worldly pleasures. It should not happen that a handful of rich people should live in jeweled palaces and the millions in miserable hovels devoid of sunlight or ventilation… In non-violent swaraj, there can be no encroachment upon just rights; contrariwise no one can possess unjust rights. In a well-organized state, usurpation should be an impossibility and it should be unnecessary to resort to force for dispossessing a usurper.

69

Decentralization

I suggest that if India is to evolve along non-violent lines, it will have to decentralize many things. Centralization cannot be sustained and defended without adequate force. Simple homes from which there is nothing to take away require no policing; the palaces of the rich must have strong guards to protect them against dacoity. So must huge factories. Rurally organized India will run less risk of foreign invasion than urbanized India well equipped with military, naval and air forces.

Centralization as a system is inconsistent with non-violent structure of society.

70

Modern State

It is not possible for a modern state based on force non-violently to resist forces of disorder, whether external or internal. A man cannot serve God and Mammon, nor be 'temperate and furious' at the same time. It is claimed that a state can be based on non-violence, i.e., it can offer non-violent resistance against a world combination based on armed force. Such a state was Ashoka's. The example can be repeated. But the case does not become weak even if it be shown that Ashoka's state was not based on non-violence. It has to be examined on its merits...

There can be no non-violence offered by the militarily strong. Thus, Russia in order to express non-violence has to discard all her power of doing violence. What is true is that if those, who were at one time strong in armed might, change their mind, they will be better able to demonstrate their non-violence to the world and, therefore, also to their opponents.

71

Violence and Terrorism

My experience teaches me that truth can never be propagated by doing violence. Those who believe in the justice of their cause have need to possess boundless patience and those alone are fit to offer civil disobedience who are above committing criminal disobedience or doing violence.

Popular violence

If I can have nothing to do with the organized violence of the government, I can have less to do with the unorganized violence of the people. I would prefer to be crushed between the two.

For me popular violence is as much an obstruction in our path as the government violence. Indeed, I can combat the government violence more successfully than the popular. For one thing, in combating the latter, I should not have the same support as in the former.

I make bold to say that violence is the creed of no religion and that, whereas non-violence in most cases is obligatory in all, violence is merely permissible in some cases. But I have not put before India the final form of non-violence.

I object to violence because, when it appears to do good, the good is only temporary; the evil it does is permanent.

72

No Faith in Violence

It is an unshakable faith with me that a cause suffers exactly to the extent that it is supported by violence. I say this in spite of appearances to the contrary. If I kill a man who abstracts me, I may experience a sense of false security. But the security will be short-lived. For I shall not have dealt with the root cause. In due course, other men will surely rise to obstruct me. My business, therefore, is not to kill the man or men who obstruct me, but to discover the cause that impels them to obstruct me and deal with it.

I do not believe in armed risings. They are a remedy worse than the disease sought to be cured. They are a token of the spirit of revenge and impatience and anger. The method of violence cannot do any good in the long run.

73

The Revolutionary

I do not deny the revolutionary's heroism and sacrifice. But heroism and sacrifice in a bad cause are so much waste of splendid energy and hurt the good cause by drawing away attention from it by the glamour of the misused heroism and sacrifice in a bad cause. I am not ashamed to stand erect before the heroic and self-sacrificing revolutionary because I am able to pit an equal measure of non-violent men's heroism and sacrifice untarnished by the blood of the innocent. Self-sacrifice of one innocent man is a million times more potent than the sacrifice of a million men who die in the act of killing others. The willing sacrifice of the innocent is the most powerful retort to insolent tyranny that has yet been conceived by God or man.

I invite the attention of the revolutionaries to the three great hindrances to swaraj—the incomplete spread of the spinning wheel, the discord between the Hindus and the Mussalmans and the inhuman ban on the suppressed classes. I ask them patiently to take their due share in this work of patient construction. It may not be spectacular enough. But on that very account, it requires all the heroic patience, silent and sustained effort and self-effacement of which the tallest among the revolutionaries is capable. Impatience will blur the revolutionary's vision and lead him astray.

Slow and inglorious self-imposed starvation among the starved masses is every time more heroic than the death on the scaffold under false exaltation.

74

Prevention of Brutalization

I am more concerned in preventing the brutalization of human nature than in the preventing of the sufferings of my own people... I know that people who voluntarily undergo a course of suffering raise themselves and the whole of humanity, but I also know that people, who become brutalized in their desperate efforts to get victory over their opponents or to exploit weaker nations or weaker men, not only drag down themselves but mankind also.

There is no necessary charm about death on the gallows; often such death is easier than a life of drudgery and toil in malicious tracts... I suggest to my friend, the revolutionary, that death on the gallows serves the country only when the victim is a 'spotless lamb'...

I do not condemn everything European. But I condemn for all climes and for all times secret murders and unfair methods even for a fair cause... Armed conspiracies against something satanic is like matching Satans against Satan. But since one Satan is one too many for me, I would not multiply him...

Cowardice, whether philosophical or otherwise, I abhor. And if I could be persuaded that revolutionary activity has dispelled cowardice, it will go a long way to soften my abhorrence of the method, however much I may still oppose it on principle... I do not regard killing or assassination or terrorism as good in any circumstances whatsoever. I do believe that ideas ripen quickly when nourished by the blood of martyrs. But a man who dies slowly of jungle fever in service bleeds as certainly as the one on the gallows. And if the one who dies on the gallows is not innocent of another's blood, he never had ideas that deserved to ripen.

75

Heroes of History

To compare their (revolutionaries') activities with those of Guru Govind Singh or Washington or Garibaldi or Lenin would be most misleading and dangerous. But, by test of the theory of non-violence, I do not hesitate to say that it is highly likely that, had I lived as their contemporary and in the respective countries, I would have called every one of them a misguided patriot, even though a successful and brave warrior...

76

Revolution Suicidal

I have not the qualifications for teaching my philosophy of life. I have barely qualifications for practising the philosophy I believe…The revolutionaries are at liberty to reject the whole of my philosophy… But India is not like Turkey or Ireland or Russia and that revolutionary activity is suicidal at this stage of the country's life at any rate, if not for all time in a country so vast, so hopelessly divided and with the masses so deeply sunk in pauperism and so fearfully terror-struck.

◆

The revolutionary destroys the body for the supposed benefit of the adversary's soul… I do not know a single revolutionary who has even thought of the adversary's soul. His single aim has been to benefit the country, even though the adversary may perish—body and soul.

◆

I honour the anarchist for his love of the country. I honour him for his bravery in being willing to die for his country; but I ask him: Is killing honorable death? I deny it.

◆

I repeat my deliberate opinion that, whatever may be true of other countries, in India at least political murder can only harm the country.

◆

The page of history is soiled red with the blood of those who have fought for freedom. I do not know an instance in which nations have attained their own without having to go through an incredible measure of travail. The dagger of the assassin, the poison bowl, the bullet of the rifle-man, the spear—and all these weapons and methods of destruction have been used up to now by what I consider blind lovers of liberty and freedom... I hold no brief for the terrorist.

◆

Let the revolutionary pray with and for me that I may soon become that (free from passions, wholly incapable of sin). But, meanwhile, let him take with me the one step to it which I see as clearly as day-light, viz. to win India's freedom with strictly non-violent means.

77

Between Cowardice and Violence

I would risk violence a thousand times rather than risk the emasculation of a whole race.

When violence is the choice

I do believe that, where there is only a choice between cowardice and violence, I would advise violence... I would rather have India resort to arms in order to defend her honour than that she should, in a cowardly manner, become or remain a helpless witness to her own dishonour. But I believe that non-violence is infinitely superior to violence, forgiveness is more manly than punishment. Forgiveness adorns a soldier. ... But abstinence is forgiveness only when there is the power to punish; it is meaningless when it pretends to proceed from a helpless creature... But I do not believe India to be helpless... I do not believe myself to be a helpless creature... Strength does not come from physical capacity. It comes from an indomitable will.

We do want to drive out the best in man, but we do not want on that account to emasculate him. And in the process of finding his own status, the beast in him is bound now and again to put up his ugly appearance.

The world is not entirely governed by logic. Life itself involves some kind of violence and we have to choose the path of least violence.

78

No Cowardice

I want both the Hindus and the Mussalmans to cultivate the cool courage to die without killing. But if one has not that courage, I want him to cultivate the art of killing and being killed rather than, in a cowardly manner, flee from danger. For the latter, in spite of his flight, does commit mental himsa. He flees because he has not the courage to be killed in the act of killing.

My method of non-violence can never lead to loss of strength, but it alone will make it possible, if the nation wills it, to offer disciplined and concerted violence in time of danger.

My creed of non-violence is an extremely active force. It has no room for cowardice or even weakness. There is hope for a violent man to be someday non-violent, but there is none for a coward. I have, therefore, said more than once... that, if we do not know how to defend ourselves, our women and our places of worship by the force of suffering, i.e., non-violence, we must, if we are men, be at least able to defend all these by fighting.

No matter how weak a person is in body, if it is a shame to flee, he will stand his ground and die at his post. This would be non-violence and bravery. No matter how weak he is, he will use what strength he has in inflicting injury on his opponent, and die in the attempt. This is bravery, but not non-violence. If, when his duty is to face danger, he flees, it is cowardice. In the first case, the man will have love or charity in him. In the second and third cases, there would be a dislike or distrust and fear.

My non-violence does admit of people, who cannot or will not be non-violent, holding and making effective use of arms. Let me repeat for the thousandth time that non-violence is of the strongest, not of the weak.

To run away from danger, instead of facing it, is to deny one's faith in man and God, even one's own self. It were better for one to drown oneself than live to declare such bankruptcy of faith.

79

Self-defence by Violence

I have been repeating over and over again that he who cannot protect himself or his nearest and dearest or their honour by non-violently facing death may and ought to do so by violently dealing with the oppressor. He who can do neither of the two is a burden. He has no business to be the head of a family. He must either hide himself, or must rest content to live forever in helplessness and be prepared to crawl like a worm at the bidding of a bully.

The strength to kill is not essential for self-defence; one ought to have the strength to die. When a man is fully ready to die, he will not even desire to offer violence. Indeed, I may put it down as a self-evident proposition that the desire to kill is in inverse proportion to the desire to die. And history is replete with instances of men who, by dying with courage and compassion on their lips, converted the hearts of their violent opponents.

Non-violence cannot be taught to a person who fears to die and has no power of resistance. A helpless mouse is not non-violent because he is always eaten by a pussy. He would gladly eat the murderess if he could, but he ever tries to flee from her. We do not call him a coward, because he is made by nature to behave no better than he does. But a man who, when faced by danger, behaves like a mouse, is rightly called a coward. He harbours violence and hatred in his heart and would kill his enemy if he could without hurting himself. He is a stranger to non-violence. All sermonizing on it will be lost on him. Bravery is foreign to his nature. Before he can understand non-violence, he has to be taught to stand his ground and even suffer death, in the attempt to defend himself against the aggressor who bids fair to overwhelm him. To do otherwise would be to confirm his cowardice and take him further away from non-violence. Whilst I may not actually help anyone to retaliate, I must not let a coward seek shelter behind non-violence so-called. Not knowing the stuff of which non-violence is made, many have honestly believed that running away from danger every time was a virtue compared to offering resistance, especially when it was fraught with danger to one's life. As a teacher of non-violence, I must, so far as it is possible for me, guard against such an unmanly belief.

◆

Self-defence is the only honourable course where there is ungreediness for self-immolation.

◆

Though violence is not lawful, when it is offered in self-defence or for the defence of the defenceless, it is an act of bravery far better than cowardly submission. The latter befits neither man nor woman. Under violence, there are many stages and varieties of bravery. Every man must judge this for himself. No other person can or has the right.

80

India and the Non-violent Way

While I admit my impotency regarding the spread of the ahimsa of the brave and the strong, as distinguished from that of the weak, the admission is not meant to imply that I do not know how the inestimable virtue is to be cultivated... It is truer (if it is a fact) to say that India is not ready for the lesson of the ahimsa of the strong than that no programme has been devised for the teaching. It will be perfectly just to say that the programme...for the ahimsa of the strong is not as attractive as that devised for the non-violence of the weak has proved to be.

81

Mere Passive Resistance

Passive resistance, unlike non-violence, has no power to change men's hearts... What is to be done to convert the poison into nectar? Is the process possible? I know that it is, and I think I know the way too. But whereas the Indian mind is ready to respond to the effort at passive resistance, it is not receptive enough to imbibe the lesson of non-violence which, and perhaps which alone, is capable of turning the poison into nectar.

Many admit that it is the way, but they have not the heart to adopt the golden path. I can proclaim from the housetop that non-violence has not, has never failed. The people failed to rise to it.

I do not mind being told that I do not know the technique of propagating non-violence. My critics even go so far as to suggest that I have no non-violence in myself. God alone knows men's hearts.

◆

It was not non-violent resistance, but passive resistance which only the weak offer because they are unable, not unwilling, to offer armed resistance. Let me make one thing clear. I have frankly and fully admitted that what we practised during the past thirty years.

If we knew the use of non-violent resistance which only those with hearts of oak can offer, we would present to the world a totally different picture of free India instead of an India cut in twain, one part highly suspicious of the other and the two too much engaged in mutual strife to be able to think cogently of the food and clothing of the hungry and naked millions, who know no religion but that of the one and only God who appears to them in the guise of the necessaries of life.

◆

It was the passivity of the weak and not the non-violence of the stout in heart, who will never surrender their sense of human unity and brotherhood even in the midst of conflict of interests, who will ever try to convert and not coerce their adversary. If India could now discover a way of sublimating the force of violence which had taken a communal turn and turning it into constructive, peaceful ways whereby differences of interests can be liquidated, it will be a great day indeed.

◆

No one has a right to say that what could not be achieved during the struggle for Independence is unachievable at all times. On the contrary, today there is a real opportunity to demonstrate the supremacy of ahimsa. True, our people have been sucked into the whirlpool of universal militarization. If even a few can keep out of it, it will be their privilege to set an example of ahimsa of the brave and be reckoned as the first servants of India. This cannot be demonstrated by intellect. Therefore, till it can be realized through experience, it must be accepted in faith.

◆

Police force

Throughout my life it has been part of my creed not to avoid the police but to assist them in prying into all my work; for I have always abhorred of secrecy and it has made my life and work easy because of my indifference to this kind of surveillance. This indifference and invariable courtesy shown to the police result in the silent conversion of several amongst them.

My indifference, however, is one thing and personal to me. As a system, the police surveillance cannot but be described as a despicable thing, unworthy of a good government. It is a useless burden upon an already over-burdened tax-payer. For, the whole of this extraordinary expenditure, it must be remembered, comes from the pockets of the toiling millions.

◆

Even in a non-violent state, a police force may be necessary. This, I admit, is a sign of my imperfect ahimsa. I have not the courage to declare that we can carry on without a police force, as I have in respect of an army. Of course, I can and do envisage a state where the police will not be necessary; but whether we shall succeed in realizing it, the future alone will show. The police of my conception will, however, be of a wholly different pattern from the present-day force. Its ranks will be composed of believers in non-violence. They will be servants, not masters, of the people. The people will instinctively render them every help, and through mutual cooperation, they will easily deal with the ever-decreasing disturbances. The police force will have some kind of arms, but they will be rarely used, if at all. In fact, the policemen will be reformers. Their police work will be confined primarily to robbers and dacoits. Quarrels between labour and capital and strikes will be few and far between in a non-violent state, because the influence of the non-violent majority will be so great as to command the respect of the principal elements in society. Similarly, there will be no room for communal disturbances.

◆

Under swaraj, you and I shall have a disciplined, intelligent police force that would keep order within and fight raiders from without, if by that time, I or someone else does not show a better way of dealing with either.

82

Crime and Punishment

In Independent India of the non-violent type, there will be crime but no criminals. They will not be punished. Crime is a disease like any other malady and is a product of the prevalent social system. Therefore, all crime including murder will be treated as a disease. Whether such an India will ever come into being is another question.

◆

What should our jails be like in free India? All criminals should be treated as patients and the jails should be hospitals admitting this class of patients for treatment and cure. No one commits crime for the fun of it. It is a sign of a diseased mind. The causes of a particular disease should be investigated and removed. They need not have palatial buildings when their jails become hospitals. No country can afford that, much less can a poor country like India. But the outlook of the jail staff should be that of physicians and nurses in a hospital. The prisoners should feel that the officials are their friends. They are there to help them to regain their mental health and not to harass them in any way. The popular governments have to issue necessary orders, but meanwhile the jail staff can do not a little to humanize their administration. What is the duty of the prisoners? ...They should behave as ideal prisoners. They should avoid breach of jail discipline. They should put their heart and soul into whatever work is entrusted to them. For instance, the prisoners' food is cooked by themselves. They should clean the rice, dal or whatever cereal is used so that there are no stones and grit or weevils in them. Whatever complaints the prisoners might have should be brought to the notice of the authorities in a becoming manner. They should so behave in their little community as to become better men when they leave the jail than when they entered it.

83

The Gospel of the Charkha

I think of the poor of India every time that I draw a thread on the wheel. The poor of India today have lost faith in God, more so than the middle classes or the rich. For a person suffering from the pangs of hunger, and desiring nothing but to fill his belly is his God. To him, anyone who gives him his bread is his master. Through him, he may even see God. To give alms to such persons, who are sound in all their limbs, is to debase oneself and them. What they need is some kind of occupation, and the occupation that will give employment to millions can only be hand-spinning...

I have described my spinning as a penance or sacrament. And, since I believe that where there is pure and active love for the poor, there is God also. I see God in every thread that I draw on the spinning wheel.

◆

The spinning wheel enables us to identify ourselves with crores. The millionaires imagine that money can bring them anything in the world. But it is not so. At any moment, death might come and snuff them out... Losing one's life...is not the same thing as shedding 'self'. One has to learn to efface self or the ego voluntarily and as a sacrifice in order to find God. The spinning wheel rules out exclusiveness. It stands for all-inclusiveness. It stands for all including the poorest. It, therefore, requires us to be humble and to cast away pride completely.

◆

Revival of *the* cottage industry, and not cottage industries, will remove the growing poverty. When once we have revived the one industry, all the other industries will follow... I would make the spinning wheel the foundation on which to build a sound village life. I would make the wheel the centre round which all other activities will revolve.

84

Message of the Charkha

I claim for the charkha the honour of being able to solve the problem of economic distress in a most natural, simple, inexpensive and business-like manner... It is the symbol of the nation's prosperity and, therefore, freedom. It is a symbol not of commercial war but of commercial peace.

◆

The message of the spinning wheel is much wider than its circumference. Its message is one of simplicity, service of mankind, living so as not to hurt others, creating an indissoluble bond between the rich and the poor, capital and labour, the prince and the peasant. That larger message is naturally for all.

◆

The message of the spinning wheel is, really, to replace the spirit of exploitation by the spirit of service. The dominant note in the West is the note of exploitation. I have no desire that our country should copy that spirit or that note.

◆

I do feel that it has message for the U.S.A. and the whole world. But it cannot be until India has demonstrated to the world that it has made the spinning wheel its own, which it has not done today. The fault is not of the wheel. I have not the slightest doubt that the saving of India and of the world lies in the wheel. If India becomes the slave of the machine, then, I say, heaven save the world?

85

Return to Simplicity

If I preach against the modern artificial life of sensual enjoyment, and ask men and women to go back to the simple life epitomized in the charkha, I do so because I know that, without an intelligent return to simplicity, there is no escape from our descent to a state lower than brutality.

◆

I believe that no other path but that of non-violence will suit India. The symbol of that dharma for India is the spinning wheel, as it alone is the friend of the distressed and the giver of plenty for the poor. The law of love knows no bounds of space or time. My swaraj, therefore, takes note of Bhangis, Dublas and the weakest of the weak, and except the spinning wheel I know no other thing which befriends all these.

86

Wheel of Life

Take to spinning [to find peace of mind]. The music of the wheel will be as balm to your soul. I believe that the yarn we spin is capable of mending the broken warp and woof of our life. The charkha is the symbol of non-violence on which all life, if it is to be real life, must be based.

◆

Some will recall through the wheel the name of that Prince of Peace, Ashoka, the founder of an empire, who ultimately gave up the pomp and circumstance of power to become the undisputed emperor of the hearts of men and became the representative of all the then-known faiths. We would call it a legitimate interpretation of the wheel to seek in it the Wheel of Law ascribed to that living store of mercy and love.

The spinning wheel, thus interpreted, adds to its importance in the life of billions of mankind. To liken it to and to derive it from the Ashoka disc is to recognize in the insignificant-looking charkha the necessity of obeying the ever-moving Wheel of the Divine Law of Love.

◆

Spinning has become a part and parcel of the ashram prayer. The conception of spinning as sacrifice has been linked with the idea of God, the reason being that we believe that in the charkha and what it stands for lies the only hope of salvation of the poor.

◆

It is my claim that the universalization of hand-spinning with a full knowledge of all that it stands for alone can bring that [conquest of inertia] in a subcontinent so vast and varied as India. I have compared spinning to the central sun and the other village crafts to the various constellations in the solar system. The former gives light and warmth to the latter and sustains them. Without it, they would not be able to exist.